✓ TREAT

Mastering Your Adult ADHD

A Cognitive-Behavioral Treatment Program

Second Edition

CLIENT WORKBOOK

STEVEN A. SAFREN
SUSAN E. SPRICH
CAROL A. PERLMAN
MICHAEL W. OTTO
EIRLY TINIFA

Copyright © 2017

First Edition published in 2005
Second Edition published in 2017

All rights reserved. No part of this book may be reproduced, translated, stored in a retrieval system, or transmitted, in any form or by any means, electronic, mechanical, photocopying, microfilming, recording, or otherwise, without written permission from the publisher.

ISBN: 9798851258558 Paperback

About Treatments That Work

One of the most difficult problems confronting patients with various disorders and diseases is finding the best help available. Everyone is aware of friends or family who have sought treatment from a seemingly reputable practitioner, only to find out later from another doctor that the original diagnosis was wrong or the treatments recommended were inappropriate or perhaps even harmful. Most patients, or family members, address this problem by reading everything they can about their symptoms, seeking out information on the Internet or aggressively "asking around" to tap knowledge from friends and acquaintances. Governments and health care policymakers are also aware that people in need do not always get the best treatments—something they refer to as *variability in health care practices*.

Now health care systems around the world are attempting to correct this variability by introducing *evidence-based practice*. This simply means that it is in everyone's interest that patients get the most up-to-date and effective care for a particular problem. Health care policymakers have also recognized that it is very useful to give consumers of health care as much information as possible, so that they can make intelligent decisions in a collaborative effort to improve physical health and mental health. This series, Treatments *That Work*, is designed to accomplish just that. Only the latest and most effective interventions for particular problems are described in user-friendly language. To be included in this series, each treatment program must pass the highest standards of evidence available, as determined by a scientific advisory board. Thus, when individuals suffering from these problems or their family members seek out an expert clinician who is familiar with these interventions and decides that they are appropriate, patients will have confidence they are receiving the best care available. Of course, only your health care professional can decide on the right mix of treatments for you.

This particular program presents the first evidence-based psychological treatment for adult attention-deficit/hyperactivity disorder (adult ADHD). In this program, you will learn skills that directly attack the symptoms that make living with adult ADHD so difficult. These symptoms include difficulty focusing attention and being easily distracted, difficulties with organization and planning, and impulsivity. This program can be effectively combined with medications, or for individuals who derive relatively little benefit from medications, this program may be sufficient on its own. This fully updated second edition of the Workbook contains worksheets, forms, and online resources to help you during treatment and is most effectively applied by working in collaboration with your clinician.

David H. Barlow, Editor-in-Chief,
Treatments *ThatWork*
Boston, MA

References

Barlow, D. H. (2004). Psychological treatments. *American Psychologist, 59*, 869–878.

Barlow, D. H. (2010). Negative effects from psychological treatments: A perspective. *American Psychologist, 65*(2), 13–20.

Institute of Medicine. (2001). *Crossing the quality chasm: A new health system for the 21st century.* Washington, DC: National Academy Press.

McHugh, R. K. & Barlow, D. H. (2010). Dissemination and implementation of evidence-based psychological interventions: A review of current efforts. *American Psychologist, 65*(2), 73–84.

Contents

Chapter 1	Information About Adult ADHD	*1*
Chapter 2	Overview of This Treatment Program for ADHD in Adulthood	*9*
Chapter 3	Informational Session with Spouse, Partner, or Family Member (if applicable)	*17*

Module 1 Organizing and Planning

Chapter 4	The Foundation: Organizing and Planning Skills	*23*
Chapter 5	Organization of Multiple Tasks	*31*
Chapter 6	Problem Solving and Managing Overwhelming Tasks	*39*
Chapter 7	Organizational Systems	*45*

Module 2 Reducing Distractibility

Chapter 8	Gauging Your Attention Span and Distractibility Delay	*53*
Chapter 9	Modifying Your Environment	*61*

Module 3 Adaptive Thinking

Chapter 10	Introducing a Cognitive Model of ADHD	*69*
Chapter 11	Adaptive Thinking	*83*
Chapter 12	Rehearsal and Review of Adaptive Thinking Skills	*93*

Module 4 Additional Skills

Chapter 13   Application of Skills to Procrastination (optional)   *99*

Chapter 14   Handling Slips   *107*

Appendix   Forms and Worksheets   *111*

References   *125*

About the Authors   *127*

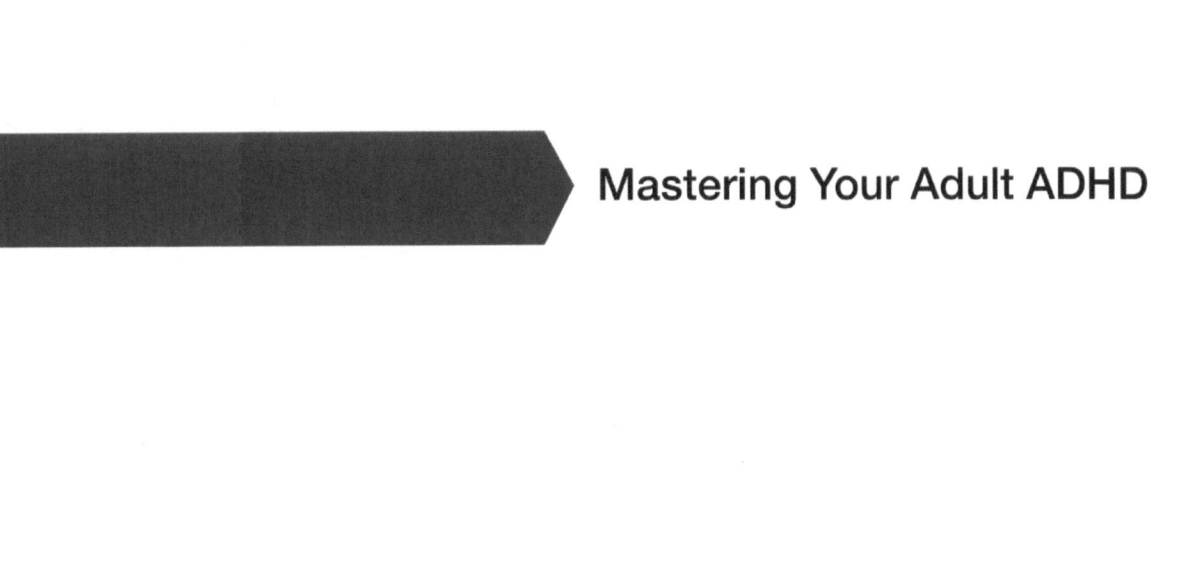# Mastering Your Adult ADHD

CHAPTER 1: Information About Adult ADHD

OVERVIEW

This chapter will provide you with information about ADHD in adulthood, how ADHD is diagnosed in adults, and an orientation to the cognitive-behavioral model of ADHD. This information will help you decide if this treatment program is right for you.

GOALS

- To understand the characteristics of ADHD in adulthood
- To learn why ADHD symptoms continue in adults even after treatment with medications
- To understand that ADHD is a valid diagnosis for adults

What Is ADHD?

Attention-deficit/hyperactivity disorder (ADHD) is a valid, medical, psychiatric disorder. ADHD begins in childhood, and many children with ADHD go on to have significant symptoms as adults. As shown in Figure 1.1, there are three major types of symptoms people have: poor attention, hyperactivity, and impulsivity.

The term **disinhibition** (lack of inhibition) is also sometimes used to describe the impulsivity and hyperactivity symptoms. Many people with ADHD have at least some symptoms of poor attention, some symptoms

SYMPTOMS OF POOR ATTENTION
Distracted easily
Difficulty organizing
Easily bored
Switch from one task to another
Difficulty planning
Difficulty concentrating
Can't do boring or unattractive tasks

SYMPTOMS OF HYPERACTIVITY
Feel like driven by a motor
Restless
Can't sit still
Always on the go
Fidgety

SYMPTOMS OF IMPULSIVITY
Interrupt often
Answer questions before person finishes asking
Blurt out inappropriate comments
Act before thinking
Do things you later regret
Difficulty waiting

Figure 1.1

Symptoms of poor attention, hyperactivity, and impulsivity

of hyperactivity, and some symptoms of impulsivity, although many people have symptoms that are predominately from one category. The term **attention deficit disorder** (ADD) is also sometimes used when an individual has the attentional symptoms but not the hyperactivity symptoms.

ADHD Is Not Related to Intelligence or Laziness

Patients with ADHD can learn coping skills to manage associated difficulties. Kate Kelly and Peggy Ramundo have written a self-help book for adults with ADHD called *You Mean I'm Not Lazy, Stupid, or Crazy?* (1993). This title underscores many of the common misperceptions that people with ADHD have about themselves.

ADHD is a neurobiological disorder, unrelated to intelligence, laziness, aptitude, being or not being crazy, and so on. This treatment program, which typically begins after an individual has been taking ADHD medications for several months, can help control the symptoms of ADHD for adults. By actively learning skills and practicing them regularly, you will see significant improvements.

What Are the Specific Criteria for a Diagnosis of ADHD?

Generally, a diagnosis of ADHD is made by a mental health professional, using the definition set forth in the American Psychiatric Association (APA)'s *Diagnostic and Statistical Manual of Mental Disorders*, 5th edition (DSM-5; 2013). The DSM-5 lists all of the various psychiatric disorders and the symptoms and other requirements that an individual must display to be diagnosed with them.

To meet the DSM-5 criteria for adult ADHD, individuals must have at least five out of the nine possible inattention symptoms and/or five out of the nine possible symptoms of hyperactivity/impulsivity. Individuals who have five or more symptoms in only the inattention category have ADHD, predominantly inattentive presentation. Those who have five or more symptoms in the hyperactivity/impulsivity category have ADHD, predominantly hyperactive/impulsive presentation. And those with five or more symptoms in both categories have ADHD, combined presentation.

Inattentive symptoms include such things as failing to give close attention to details, difficulty sustaining attention in tasks, seeming not to listen when being spoken to directly, failure to follow through on instructions, difficulties with organization, avoidance of tasks that require sustained mental effort, frequently losing things, getting distracted easily, and being forgetful.

Hyperactive/impulsive symptoms include fidgeting, leaving one's seat frequently, feelings of restlessness, being unable to engage in quiet activities, being "on the go," talking excessively, blurting out answers, having difficulty waiting in lines, and frequently interrupting.

In addition, (1) the person needs to have had at least some of the symptoms before the age of 12, (2) the symptoms need to be present in at least two different settings, (3) the symptoms need to clearly interfere with the individual's ability to function, and (4) it must be clear that the symptoms are not better accounted for by a different mental disorder (APA, 2013).

How Do We Distinguish ADHD as a Diagnosis from Normal Functioning?

Some of the symptoms listed above sound like they might apply to almost anyone at certain times. For example, most people would probably say that they are sometimes easily distracted or sometimes have problems organizing. This is actually the case with many of the psychiatric disorders. For example, everyone gets sad sometimes, but not everyone meets criteria for a clinical diagnosis of depression. To qualify for a diagnosis of ADHD, the person must have significant difficulties with some aspect of his or her life, such as work, school, or relationships. In DSM-5, there is more attention to impairment specific to adults, such as impairment in work situations.

Also, to qualify for the diagnosis, the person's distress and impairment must be caused by ADHD and not by another disorder. A thorough assessment is needed to rule out the possibility that the symptoms reflect another psychiatric disorder.

How Do Cognitive and Behavioral Variables Make ADHD Worse for Adults?

Cognitive components (thoughts and beliefs) can worsen ADHD symptoms. For example, a person who is facing something that he will find overwhelming might shift his attention elsewhere, or think things like, "I can't do this," "I don't want to do this," or "I will do this later." *Behavioral components* are the things people do that can make ADHD symptoms worse. The actual behaviors can include things like avoiding doing what you should be doing or keeping or not keeping an organizational system.

Later in this chapter, we show a model of how we believe ADHD affects the lives of adults. According to this model, the core symptoms of ADHD are biologically based. However, we believe that cognitive and behavioral variables also affect symptom levels.

Core neuropsychiatric impairments, starting in childhood, prevent effective coping. By definition, adults with ADHD have been suffering from this disorder chronically since childhood. Specific symptoms such as distractibility, disorganization, difficulty following through on tasks, and impulsivity can prevent people with ADHD from learning or using effective coping skills.

Because of these symptoms, individuals with this disorder typically have sustained underachievement, or other experiences that they might label as "failures." In turn, this history of failures can result in people with ADHD developing overly negative beliefs about themselves, as well as negative, maladaptive thinking when approaching tasks. The negative thoughts and beliefs that ensue can therefore add to avoidance or distractibility. Therefore, people with ADHD shift their attention even more when confronted with tasks or problems that they may find difficult or boring, and related behavioral symptoms can also get worse.

A model of how these factors interrelate is presented in Figure 1.2.

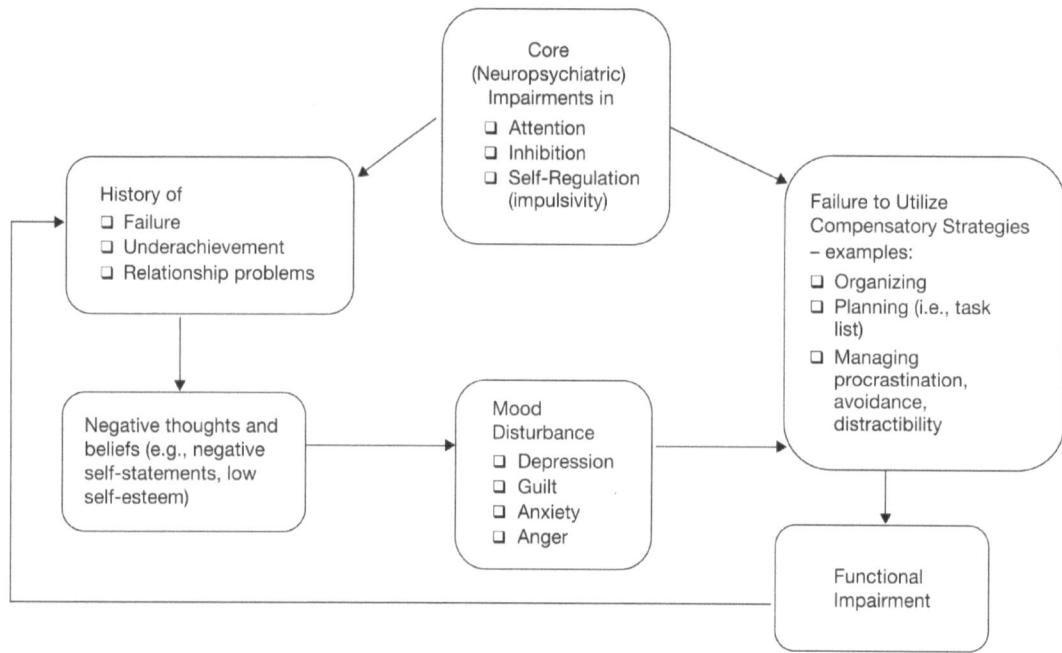

Figure 1.2

Cognitive-behavioral model of adult ADHD

Reprinted from S. A. Safren, S. Sprich, S. Chulvick, & M. W. Otto (2004). Psychosocial treatments for adults with ADHD. *Psychiatric Clinics of North America, 27*(2), 349–360, © 2004 Elsevier Inc., with permission from Elsevier.

Don't Medications Effectively Treat ADHD?

Yes. Medications are currently the first-line treatment approach for adult ADHD, and they are the most extensively studied. The classes of these medications are stimulants, tricyclic antidepressants, monoamine oxidase inhibitors (antidepressants), and atypical antidepressants. However, a good number of individuals (approximately 20% to 50%) who take antidepressants are considered nonresponders. A nonresponder is an individual whose symptoms are not sufficiently reduced, or someone who cannot tolerate the medications. Additionally, adults who are considered responders typically show a reduction in only 50% or less of the core symptoms of ADHD.

Because of these data, recommendations for the best treatment of adult ADHD include using psychotherapy (cognitive-behavioral therapy in particular) with medications. Medications can reduce many of the core symptoms of ADHD: attentional problems, high activity, and impulsivity.

You may be asking yourself why this treatment program is needed in addition to medications. The answer is that medications alone cannot provide adults with ADHD with concrete strategies and skills for coping. Furthermore, disruptions resulting from ADHD, such as underachievement, unemployment or underemployment, economic problems, and relationship difficulties, call for additional interventions to improve the person's quality of life.

ADHD in Adulthood Is a Real and Valid Medical Condition

We are including this section here in this client workbook because in the recent past, ADHD was a controversial diagnosis. However, the past several decades of study have shown that its validity is now strong. Here we will describe the controversy regarding the diagnosis and outline the evidence that has led experts to conclude that adult ADHD is a prevalent, distressing, impairing, and valid medical diagnosis.

Psychiatric and Psychological Diagnoses Are Difficult to Validate Compared to Other Biomedical Diseases

ADHD in adulthood is a real, reliably diagnosed medical illness that may affect up to 5% of the adults in the United States. ADHD in adulthood has historically been a controversial diagnosis. One of the reasons for this is that psychiatric diagnoses, in general, are difficult to validate. In many other medical fields, doctors can perform a blood test, do an x-ray, take a biopsy, or even take a patient's temperature to help make a diagnosis. In these cases, overt medical evidence complements the report of the patient. However, for psychiatric disorders, this is impossible at present. Doctors must diagnose psychiatric disorders based only on their patient's self-report of their symptoms, their own observation of the patient, or the observations of others. Therefore, psychiatrists and psychologists have developed a way to categorize psychiatric disorders that involves looking at groups of symptoms that people have.

How Do Doctors Validate Psychological or Psychiatric Diagnoses?

To validate a psychiatric or psychological diagnosis, psychologists and psychiatrists examine data such as the degree to which trained individuals agree on the diagnosis, the degree to which the disorder runs in families (including adoption studies to determine the relative impact of biology vs. environment), any neuroimaging and neurochemistry studies, and the degree to which people who have the problem experience distress. This has been done sufficiently for adult ADHD.

How Do We Know That ADHD Is a "Real" Diagnosis?

Sufficient scientific evidence has accumulated over the past several decades leading toward the finding that ADHD is a real, significant, distressing, interfering, and legitimate medical problem. This includes evidence that ADHD can be reliably diagnosed in adults and that the diagnosis meets standards of diagnostic validity similar to those of other psychiatric diagnoses. Accordingly, core symptoms in adulthood include impairments in attention, inhibition, and self-regulation. These core symptoms lead to impairments in adulthood, such as the following:

- *Poor school and work performance* (e.g., difficulty with organization or planning, becoming easily bored, deficient sustained attention to reading and paperwork, procrastination, poor time management, impulsive decision making)
- *Impaired interpersonal skills* (e.g., problems with friendships, poor follow-through on commitments, poor listening skills, difficulty with intimate relationships)
- *Behavior problems* (e.g., individuals with ADHD are less educated than predicted based on ability, difficulties with financial management, trouble organizing one's home, chaotic routines)

There is further evidence for the validity of ADHD as a diagnosis from medication treatment studies, genetic studies that include adoption and family studies, and neuroimaging and neurochemistry research.

Children with ADHD Do Grow Up

It is estimated that between 1% and 5% of adults have ADHD. This is consistent with estimates that ADHD affects 2% to 9% of school-age children, and follow-up studies of children diagnosed with ADHD show that impairing ADHD symptoms persist into adulthood (beyond adolescence) in 30% to 80% of diagnosed children.

Conclusion

Now that you have learned about adult ADHD and this treatment program, you are ready to begin! You have already taken a big step by purchasing this workbook and making the decision to participate in this program. Let's get started!

CHAPTER 2 — Overview of This Treatment Program for ADHD in Adulthood

OVERVIEW

This chapter will provide information about how this program was developed to address the specific concerns of adults with ADHD who are treated with medications. The chapter will also provide information about the success of the program in addressing these concerns and additional information about exactly what the program will entail.

GOALS

- To learn how this program was developed
- To learn about the concerns of medication-treated adults with ADHD
- To understand the success rate of the program so far
- To understand what the program will involve

This treatment program is meant to be completed with the assistance of a cognitive-behavioral therapist. The treatment was developed by the Massachusetts General Hospital's Cognitive-Behavioral Therapy Program. It was based on the clinical experience of the authors, input from adults with ADHD, and published works on treatment for adults with ADHD (e.g., Barkley, 1998; Hallowell, 1995; Mayes, 1998; McDermott, 2000; Nadeau, 1995). It is designed for individuals who have been diagnosed with ADHD, have been on medications for ADHD, and have found a stable medication regimen. The strategies may be useful for adults with ADHD who cannot take medications, but we have only tested it for individuals who were already taking medications.

How Was the Program Developed?

Clinical Experience of the Authors

The program was developed by a group of psychologists at Massachusetts General Hospital and Harvard Medical School after treating patients with ADHD in our clinic using cognitive-behavioral therapy. From this perspective, it was originally developed based on our clinical experience, the general principles of cognitive-behavioral therapy, and published clinical guidelines for working with adult patients with ADHD.

Input from Adults with ADHD

Patients with ADHD also gave input to the development of the treatment program. One of us interviewed a group of patients with ADHD who had been taking medications about the types of problems they were experiencing and what they felt would be helpful regarding cognitive-behavioral treatment.

The most frequently discussed problems among adult patients with ADHD who had been taking medicines were (1) organizing and planning, (2) distractibility, and (3) associated anxiety and depression. Other concerns included problems with procrastination, anger management, and communication issues.

Organizing and Planning

Problems with *organizing and planning* involve difficulties figuring out the logical, discrete steps to complete tasks that seem overwhelming. For many clients, this difficulty leads to giving up, procrastination, anxiety, and feelings of incompetence and underachievement. For example, several of our clients who were underemployed or unemployed had never completed thorough job searches, so they did not have a job, were working in much lower-paying positions than they could have been, or were not working at a job that would lead to appropriate employment.

Distractibility

The problems with *distractibility* involved problems in work or school. Many of our clients have reported that they do not complete tasks because other, less important things get in the way. Examples might include sitting down at one's computer to work on a project, but constantly going on the Internet to look up certain websites or browsing social networking sites. One student in our program told us that whenever he sat down to work on his thesis, he would find another place in his apartment to clean (even though it was already basically clean enough).

Mood Problems (Associated Anxiety and Depression)

Secondary to core ADHD symptoms, many of our clients have mood problems. These problems involve worry about events in their lives, and sadness regarding either real or perceived underachievement. Many individuals with ADHD report a strong sense of frustration about tasks that they do not finish, or do not do as well as they feel that they could have.

Has This Program Been Successful?

Yes! In our study of this treatment, we found that people who completed this program in addition to taking their medications did significantly better than people who stayed on their medications but did not receive this treatment (Safren, Otto, Sprich, Winett, Wilens, & Biederman, 2005).

We conducted a "randomized controlled trial" to find these results. Randomized controlled trials are a primary way researchers test whether treatments work. They are called *randomized* because patients entering the study randomly receive either the treatment or a control condition. In our study we only took in patients with ADHD who were being treated with medications and still had significant problems. These patients were randomized to either getting the treatment described in this book or no additional treatment. (All patients continued taking their prescribed medications.)

In this study, the people who got the treatment had significantly lower symptoms of ADHD after the treatment. This was evaluated by an independent assessor who did not know whether the participants got the treatment or not, and by the self-report of participants who completed written questionnaires about their symptoms. According to these assessments, patients who went through the program experienced about a 50% decrease in symptoms, and those who did not had negligible changes.

Later, we conducted a larger five-year study funded by a grant from the National Institute of Mental Health (to Dr. Safren), also using the first version of our treatment manual. This study involved comparing the treatment in this manual plus continued medications to a comparison treatment (relaxation plus educational support) plus continued medications (Safren, Sprich, Mimiaga, Surman, Knouse, Groves, & Otto, 2010). Eighty-six adults with ADHD participated in this study. We found that participants receiving cognitive-behavioral treatment achieved lower scores on measures of ADHD compared with participants receiving the comparison treatment, and there were more responders in the cognitive-behavioral treatment group than the comparison group. This means that more people in the cognitive-behavioral treatment group were considered significantly improved than in the comparison group. These gains were maintained at six- and 12-month follow-up.

What Will the Program Entail?

Regular Meetings with a Therapist and Home Practice

The treatment involves regular meetings with a cognitive-behavioral therapist and home practice assignments. We have found that weekly sessions work best. By having weekly sessions, you have a chance to practice the skills discussed in the treatment every week. Also, there is a relatively short period of time between sessions so that any problems with follow-through can be solved, and any questions about the approach can be answered. When we have conducted sessions every other week, clients reported that it was difficult because they would forget what they were supposed to be doing on their own.

The treatment is different than traditional psychotherapy. In fact, in some ways it is more like taking a course than being in supportive psychotherapy. Each session will have an agenda, and each session will have an associated home practice assignment.

Practice Is Essential

The program involves practicing outside of the sessions: There are no two ways about it! We have found that many clients have tried similar strategies in the past but have had difficulties integrating this practice into their daily lives. In other words, the tendency to be distractible and forgetful can get in the way of treatment. We will work with you to "set in" new habits that you can keep with you over the years

> **You will need to practice these new skills long enough for them to become a habit—for them to be easy to use and remember.**

Do Not Quit

You may be tempted to quit, but not at the beginning when things will be exciting and new and therefore more interesting. People typically do not quit at the beginning. The middle period can sometimes be the hardest. This is when the novelty wears off, but people have not practiced the skills long enough for them to become habits. Many people show some improvement at the beginning, enough so they start to think that they do not need to use the skills. In this case, people may quit (because it is no longer new and interesting, and is not yet an easy habit), but then they relapse back to having problems, and then think, "I tried to change and I could not do it." Hence, the cycle of negative emotions and continued ADHD symptoms persists.

> **Do not succumb to this temptation!**

This may be the hardest part of the treatment program. The key to getting better is to stay on track and stick with the program long enough for it to become easier. There will be ups and downs over the course of treatment. But when there is a "down," this is definitely not the time to quit. Rather, this is the time to learn from the things that led up to the setback, and figure out how to handle them in the future. This is extremely important.

> **Setbacks are a major part of progress. You need to have setbacks and learn to handle them in order to reduce the likelihood of future setbacks!**

The final period is likely to be easier, but it can also entail challenges. Once you start seeing improvements, you will be faced with the challenge of continuing to invest some time and energy in maintaining these systems and skills even though things are going better. We have found that some people, once they are doing better, feel less motivated to keep using the coping skills. If things are bad, then there is more motivation because people feel that the need to "get out of the hole." But when things are going well, some people lose their motivation—and this can lead to setbacks.

The Three Modules of the Program

Organization and Planning

The first part of the treatment involves organization and planning skills. This includes skills such as the following:

- Learning to effectively and consistently use a calendar
- Learning to effectively and consistently use a task list
- Working on effective problem-solving skills, such as breaking down tasks into steps and choosing a best solution for a problem when no solution is ideal
- Developing a triage system for mail and papers
- Developing organizational systems for papers, electronic files, and other items

Managing Distractibility

The second part of treatment involves managing distractibility. Skills include the following:

- Determining a reasonable length of time that you can expect to focus on boring or difficult tasks, and then breaking tasks down into chunks that match this length of time
- Using a timer, cues, and other techniques (e.g., distractibility delay)

Cognitive Restructuring (Adaptive Thinking)

The third part of treatment involves learning to think about problems and stressors in the most adaptive way possible. This includes the following:

- Positive "self-coaching"
- Learning how to identify and dispute negative and/or unhelpful thoughts

- Learning how to look at situations rationally, and therefore make rational choices about the best possible solutions
- Learning how to identify and change "overly positive" thinking patterns

Procrastination

An optional additional module exists for procrastination. We include this because even though most of the previous modules do relate to procrastination, some people require extra help in this area. This module therefore focuses on how to use the skills above to help with procrastination.

Monitoring Progress

before starting this program, your therapist will likely have done a diagnostic interview to establish whether or not you have ADHD. Part of the treatment approach described in this workbook involves regularly monitoring your improvement. Because, unlike many medical illnesses, we do not have a blood test for symptom severity, we need to use the next best thing, which is the Adult ADHD Self-Report Scale (ASRS) Symptom Checklist (https://www.hcp.med.harvard.edu/ncs/ftpdir/adhd/18Q_ASRS_English.pdf). Your therapist will give you a copy to fill out at the start of each session.

Agendas for Treatment Sessions

To ensure that important material is covered, you and your therapist will set an agenda for each therapy session.

One potential pitfall with modular treatment is that not everything can be covered at once. Although the treatment approach is offered one module at a time, you may have areas of difficulty that will not be addressed until future sessions. This is an issue that is sometimes frustrating for clients. The program typically starts with the development of a calendar and task list system. That module also involves learning organization and planning skills. The next module targets distractibility. People sometimes have problems with the first module because they get easily distracted, but distractibility is not covered until the next module. We ask that you do your best, but we also realize that you will not have learned all the necessary skills until the end of the treatment program.

Repeating Information

There are many areas of the treatment where we repeat key information. We do this because repetition is the best way to learn new information. Each module contains new information and also contains information from previous modules that is important to review.

Remembering to Take Medication

For some people with ADHD, taking medication every day, sometimes more than once a day, can be difficult. Symptoms of ADHD such as distractibility or poor organization may interfere, causing you to forget to take all of your prescribed doses or to have difficulty developing a structured routine for taking medication. This treatment will help you prioritize taking medication and will provide you with opportunities to work with a therapist and try to resolve any difficulties you have taking medications. Each week you will discuss factors leading to missed doses and will try to come up with a plan to avoid this in the future.

CHAPTER 3: Informational Session with Spouse, Partner, or Family Member (if applicable)

OVERVIEW

This chapter will assist you in working with a spouse, partner, or family member to better manage your ADHD symptoms. As has been discussed earlier, this treatment program is best done with the aid of a therapist who is familiar with cognitive-behavioral therapy. We therefore recommend that you and your family member meet with the therapist for one session to go over the material presented in the first two chapters, and to deal with any other information that may be pertinent.

> ***NOTE:*** *This session can take place at any time between Sessions 2 and 6. The primary goals are to provide information about the treatment to your family member and to make sure that everyone is "on the same page" about the treatment. You can talk with your therapist about what makes the most sense in terms of the treatment and you can talk with your family member about his or her schedule and then plan accordingly.*

Involving a family member in treatment will enable you to do the following:

- To gain support as you complete treatment
- To decrease tension in your relationship related to ADHD symptoms

GOALS

- To provide education about ADHD
- To provide an overview of the cognitive-behavioral model of the continuation of ADHD into adulthood
- To discuss organization and planning techniques
- To discuss techniques for coping with distractibility
- To discuss adaptive thinking techniques
- To discuss involvement of your family member in the treatment
- To discuss ways that your family member can help and support the treatment

Symptom Severity Scale

As you have been doing each week, complete the ASRS Symptom Checklist at the start of your therapy session, and share this information with your therapist.

Score: _____   Date: _____

Medication Adherence

Record your prescribed dosage of medication and indicate the number of doses you missed. Review triggers for missed doses such as distractibility, running out of medication, or thoughts about not wanting/needing to take medication.

Prescribed doses per week: _____

Doses missed this week: _____

Triggers for missed doses:

_____

_____

Review of Previously Presented Material

The information presented in the earlier chapters of this workbook can be shared with your family member. This information lays the groundwork for the remaining sessions. We recommend that this be discussed with your cognitive-behavioral therapist, who can answer questions that your family member might have.

Monitoring Progress

Each week we monitor progress by completing the ASRS Symptom Checklist. We find that this is helpful to identify areas that are most problematic and areas that should be targeted for additional work. We also sometimes ask the partner or family member to complete the ASRS Symptom Checklist as a secondary way to report on progress. If you are willing, we would like to have your family member complete one, and we can compare ratings to see if problematic areas are similar.

Practice

- Continue to discuss ways in which your family member can provide support while you are in treatment.
- Read over the materials for the next session.

MODULE 1

Organizing and Planning

CHAPTER 4: The Foundation: Organizing and Planning Skills

OVERVIEW

This chapter will help you come up with goals for therapy that are both specific and within your control. In addition, you will learn the foundational skills that will allow you to get started with your own personalized task list and calendar systems.

GOALS

- To understand the severity of your initial symptoms as a basis for tracking treatment progress
- To discuss realistic goals
- To learn about the modular approach to treatment, and the importance of practice, motivation, and staying with it
- To be introduced to using task list and calendar systems
- To get started with task list and calendar systems

Symptom Checklist

At the start of each session, your therapist will give you a copy of the ASRS Symptom Checklist to complete. This checklist lists each of the diagnostic symptoms of ADHD, so that you can rate yourself. Each week of treatment will involve targeting specific symptoms from this assessment. As you go through the treatment, you should expect to see a gradual decline in symptom severity. If there are specific sets of symptoms that do not seem to be changing, these are areas on which you should focus.

Tracking your symptoms on a weekly basis can also help you become more aware of these difficulties. Being aware that these are symptoms of ADHD, doing this self-assessment on a weekly basis, and tracking the changes can also be helpful on its own. This awareness can help you remember to use the skills that you will be learning in the sessions that follow.

Complete the ASRS Symptom Checklist now. Pay particular attention to the items that have the highest ratings, as these should be targets for treatment. Then fill in your score and today's date in the lines here:

Score: _____   Date: _____

Medication Adherence

Record your prescribed dosage of medication and indicate the number of doses you missed. Review triggers for missed doses such as distractibility, running out of medication, or thoughts about not wanting/needing to take medication. Repeat this exercise before every therapy session and share it with your therapist so that it can be discussed in therapy.

Prescribed doses per week: _____

Doses missed this week: _____

Triggers for missed doses:

_____

_____

Goals for Cognitive-Behavioral Therapy for ADHD

You have just completed a checklist of the symptoms that are typical of ADHD in adults. We find that reviewing this list can also help you think about individual goals that you might have regarding which types of problems most affect you. Additionally, it might help you think about how they actually interfere in your life.

Part of getting started on this course of cognitive-behavioral therapy (CBT) for ADHD is making sure you have realistic goals for the treatment. Realistic goals are things that you can control.

Realism and Controllability

You might be thinking that a long-term (or medium-term) goal of yours is to get a better job. This is a great goal, and we believe the skills described in this workbook can help you increase the chances of getting a better job. However, the outcome of getting a better job is dependent on lots of other factors that you do not directly control (e.g., the economy and the availability of the types of jobs you want). A realistic goal would therefore be to figure out what steps are necessary to improve the chances of getting a better job, and then acting on these steps.

There are likely areas related to ADHD that are also preventing you from getting a better job. Steps related to overcoming these might include figuring out an effective job search process, improving your organizational skills at work, and improving your productivity. These are issues that the treatment can help with because we can directly control them.

Questions to Help Come Up with Goals

The following questions may help you come up with goals regarding your treatment:

- What made you decide to start this treatment now?
- What types of things would you like to be different regarding how you approach tasks?
- What are some issues that others have noticed about how you approach things?
- If you did not have problems with ADHD, what do you think would be different in your life?

In Figure 4.1, write down your goals for CBT. There are also columns for controllability, and whether the goal is a short- or long-term one. For controllability, write down how much control you think you have over this goal even if the ADHD symptoms were gone (0% represents no

Goal of CBT	Controllability (as a percent)	Short or Long term

Figure 4.1

Goals for cognitive-behavioral therapy

control; 100% represents complete control). Also indicate whether this is a short-term or long-term goal.

We ask you to rate controllability (and this should be done with a therapist) so that you can gain a realistic appraisal of your goals for CBT. For example, a goal might be to move to a new house. However, there are many factors involved in moving to a new house, such as the state of the housing market in your area, and whether you get approved for a mortgage quickly. Hence, we prefer to have a related goal that is more controllable—for example, do the tasks necessary to optimize the chances of moving to a new house.

Re-review the goals, and the controllability ratings. Ask yourself if there are specific areas that you can control about each situation, and if there are specific areas that are beyond your control.

Information About the Modular Approach to Treatment

As we have discussed, this treatment is modular. In other words, it is designed so that each skill builds upon previously learned skills. You will be learning one technique at a time. As you begin this treatment program, there are several things to keep in mind about how the treatment is structured.

The Therapy Is Active

First, due to difficulties known to be associated with ADHD, the therapy will be especially active, almost like taking a course. Each session will have an agenda that you and your therapist will discuss at the beginning.

The Therapy Requires Practice Outside of Sessions

Each session will involve a review of the things you have already learned and are working on, as well as discussing new coping strategies and trying them out for the next week. The more you are able to do this, the better the results you will see.

The Therapy Works on One Skill at a Time

This means that you will have areas of difficulty that are not addressed right away. For example, the first module is on organizing and planning. The second is on distractibility. Of course, organizing and planning things are much easier if you do not become distracted. Likewise, if we started with distractibility, it would be difficult to figure out what you were getting distracted from if you are not organized. Therefore, it is important to realize that only one thing at a time can be changed, and the key is to practice things long enough so that you can really tell if they will be helpful to you.

Practice Makes Perfect

You are about to start a treatment for problems that involve difficulties with follow-through. Some or all of these skills may seem difficult. This is why you will be doing the treatment with a therapist and not on your own, and this is also why it is critical to know right from the start how important it is to practice these new skills. Remember the model of cognitive-behavioral therapy for ADHD that is presented in Figure 1.2 in Chapter 1 of this workbook. Many people with ADHD never get a chance to learn coping skills because they quit practicing a skill before they have practiced it enough for it to become a habit!

Motivation Is Key

> **If you participate in this program, there will certainly be challenges. It can be difficult to maintain your motivation.**

Your therapist will be working with you to help you understand exactly how each skill may be useful for you. Your therapist will also be working to make sure that you are working on goals that are important for you. Be sure to give your therapist feedback if there are times when you are not clear about how a particular skill might be useful for you, or if you are feeling that your therapist does not understand your goals. By doing this, you can get the most out of the treatment program.

Skill: Using a Calendar and Task List

Calendar and task list systems are the foundation of organization. These are absolutely necessary. Although there are other things you also need in order to be organized, these things are critical.

We consider it akin to eating for health maintenance. To maintain your health, you need to be able to eat. However, there are many other things that you also need to do to maintain your health, such as going to the doctor, taking medicine if you get an infection, and so on. Eating is a necessary—but not sufficient—requirement for health. We believe that calendar and task list systems are necessary—but not sufficient—requirements for being organized.

Using the Calendar and Task List Together

The calendar system and task list systems can be personalized, even though we give specific recommendations. Many individuals report that they have tried to use a calendar system in the past but it has not worked, or they did not keep up with it. Remember, the goal of this treatment is to try things long enough for them to become automatic habits. Every session from here on out involves tasks that build on the use of the calendar and task list system. These two items can be used together.

- *The task list* will contain information that you need but that is not tied to a specific date. The task list should replace having random pieces of paper that can be easily lost.
- *The calendar* is your key to appointments. When using the calendar with the task list, you may place items from the task list onto specific days or times.

Rules for the Calendar and Task List

1. **The calendar and task list system replaces ALL pieces of paper.**
   - Pieces of paper just get lost.
   - Instead of keeping an appointment slip, a business card, or anything like this, copy the information onto the task list or enter it directly on your calendar.
2. **Phone messages from voice mail or other places go on the task list.**
   - Log every phone message (from voice mail and so forth) on the task list as a *to-do* item.
   - If you date when you have completed the task, you will then have a record of having done it in case anyone asks you about it in the future.
3. **All appointments go on the calendar.**
   - No appointment slips that can easily get lost!
4. **All tasks must go on the task list.**
   - The task list is something that will be further developed in future chapters. This is a key component of the program.
   - Task list items should be looked at EVERY DAY, and revised accordingly.
5. **Do not obsess about trying to get a perfect system.**
   - Many individuals want to have the perfect calendar and task list systems. Do not fall into this trap! This will just result in not having any systems.
   - If you cannot decide on the "best" system, then just use a simple calendar and task list system.
   - Remember, it's important to give your system a fair shot! This means keeping one system for at least three months, long enough to get used to it.

6. **Use a system that is within your comfort zone.**
    - There are many, many options for different calendar and task list systems—including paper systems, applications on smartphones or tablets, and multiple computerized applications. Many of our clients ask us which is the "best" system, and this is not really a question that we can easily answer. The question for you to ask yourself is this: "What is the best system for me?"

If you are not proficient at computers or smartphone applications, you can always try to become proficient at these things at the end of this treatment. We recommend, however, that this be a separate goal from this program.

Potential Pitfalls

It is important to remember that learning any new skill takes practice and it takes time. You may not be used to writing down appointments or carrying around your task list and calendar systems. Be aware of thoughts that may sabotage your success down the road, such as these:

"I don't have room in my bag for my tablet or smartphone."

"I've never been an organized person; why start now?"

"If I write down my appointments and assignments, I will then be responsible for them."

In later chapters you will be learning ways to manage these interfering thoughts. For now, try to keep focused on your reasons for beginning this program, the goals you hope to achieve, and the sense of accomplishment you will feel for taking positive steps in your life.

Practice

- Create an organizational system with a calendar and a task list following the rules above.
- Put all appointments on the calendar and start ONE master task list.
- Read over the materials for the next session.

CHAPTER 5: Organization of Multiple Tasks

OVERVIEW

The main focus of this chapter is to teach you how to manage multiple tasks. It is important for you to remember that practice makes perfect.

Although these techniques may seem unfamiliar at first, over time they will become more automatic. Even if you feel frustrated, stick with the techniques until they become habits.

GOALS

- To continue to monitor your progress
- To review your use of the calendar and task list
- To learn how to manage multiple tasks
- To learn how to prioritize tasks
- To problem solve regarding any anticipated difficulties using this technique
- To identify exercises for home practice

Review of Symptom Checklist

As you have been doing each week, complete the ASRS Symptom Checklist at the start of your therapy session, and share this information with your therapist.

Score: _____   Date: _____

Review of Medication Adherence

As you have been doing each week, record your prescribed dosage of medication and indicate the number of doses you missed. Review triggers for missed doses such as distractibility, running out of medication, or thoughts about not wanting/needing to take medication.

Prescribed doses per week: _____

Doses missed this week: _____

Triggers for missed doses:

_____

_____

Review of Previous Chapters

Each week you should examine your progress in implementing the skills that you have learned so far in this treatment. It is important to acknowledge the successes you have achieved and to try to resolve any difficulties.

To review, the tools for organization and planning are as follows:

- Use of calendar for managing appointments
- Use of task list system

Remember, having a good calendar and task list system is NECESSARY (but not sufficient) to getting organized.

If you have not yet decided on systems to use to keep track of your appointments and tasks, this should be your top priority. Problem-solving skills are covered in future sessions, but before that, try to solve any problems you have getting started with your systems. Remember: For this approach to be successful, you need to have the proper tools!

If you have initiated the use of calendar and task list systems, review the specifics:

- How will you remember to look at your calendar every day?
- How will you remember to look at your task list every day? (We find that picking a time every day is the best—for example, when you feed your dog, after you brush your teeth, or while you are having your morning coffee or breakfast.)

Remember, just because you have a task list, it doesn't mean that you have to complete all of the items on the list immediately! It is simply a tool that is going to help you become organized and avoid forgetting things that are not on the list.

> **The calendar and task lists are building blocks for the rest of the treatment program. Make sure to plan a strategy to look at them EVERY DAY!**

Managing Multiple Tasks

When looking at the task list and the calendar, you may have noticed that we often need to manage multiple tasks at one time.

When you have ADHD, it can become difficult to decide which task is most important. Even if you have decided that a particular task is important, it is often difficult to stick with it until it is completed.

In the following exercise, you will learn a concrete strategy to help you decide which tasks are most important. This technique is one example of how you can "force yourself" to organize tasks, even though it is difficult for people with ADHD to process this type of information.

Master List Versus Daily List

It is important to have both a "master list" that holds all of the tasks that need to be completed, in general, and a "daily list" of tasks that you are actually hoping to complete on a particular day. You can divide the list up into different sections, such as home projects and work projects, if desired.

All tasks should remain on the master list until they have been completed. If you do not complete a task on the daily list that day, move it to the next day's list. Many electronic systems allow items to be assigned a particular date, and the item will automatically move to the following day if it has not been checked off as having been completed. This can also be done using a paper system.

Skill: Prioritizing

When you are faced with a number of tasks that you must do, it is important to have a clear strategy for prioritizing which tasks are most important, so that the most important tasks are sure to get completed. The best way that we know of to do this is to rate each task.

We find that people like to complete the tasks that are easier first. This can be problematic because the easier tasks are often the tasks that are not as important. When we do this, we get the feeling that we are getting things accomplished, but we find that we are never making progress on our important goals.

Skill: The A, B, C's

List all of your tasks. Then assign an "A," "B," or "C" rating to each task:

- **"A" Tasks:** These are the tasks of highest importance. They must be completed in the short term (like today or tomorrow).
- **"B" Tasks:** These are lower-importance, longer-term tasks. Some portions should be completed in the short term, but other portions may take longer.
- **"C" Tasks:** These are the tasks of lowest importance. They may be more attractive and easier to do, but they are not as important.

Work with your therapist to generate a task list, and discuss ratings for each item. Be very careful not to rate too many items as "A"!

This rating strategy can be applied both to the master list and to the daily list. In the case of the master list, you can use it to decide which items are most important and need to go on that day's list. In the case of the daily list, you would use it to decide which item to do first, which to do second, and so on.

You can see that the priority ratings are not static. For example, a task that needs to be completed in the distant future may be placed on your master list, and you might rate it as a "C." However, as the deadline approaches, you may change the rating to a "B" and then finally an "A" if you have not yet completed it. Sometimes, events will occur that may cause you to modify your ratings (e.g., an email from your boss asking about the report you were supposed to write).

Skill: Using This Technique

You can now add this technique to the toolbox of skills you are developing to combat your ADHD symptoms. In addition to making a "to do" list for each day, you should now assign a rating of "A," "B," or "C" to each task. You should do *all* of the "A" tasks before doing *any* of the "B" tasks! This may be hard for you, but it is very important! It will help you to make sure that you complete the tasks that are important to you.

Use this technique every day. Get in the habit of pausing to assess what you need to do and to carefully decide what you should start with, what you should do second, and so on. By practicing this technique regularly, you will ensure that the most important tasks get completed.

Potential Pitfalls

You may be feeling that we are asking you to do a lot, but don't get discouraged! You are trying to learn some new skills, and it will take some time before the skills become habits. As you become more accustomed to using your task list, you will learn more about how much is realistic for you to expect to do in one day.

At this point, if you find that you are not finishing all of the items on your list, simply re-rate them the next day. In later chapters, you may want to use some problem-solving techniques if you are finding that you are consistently not finishing the most important items on your list.

Remember, at this point, you are just trying to get in the habit of using the task list.

Practice

- Put all appointments on the calendar and review the task list on a daily basis.
- Use and look at the task list and calendar EVERY DAY!
- Select items from the master list to put on the daily task list.
- Rate each task as an "A," "B," or "C" task.
- Practice doing all of the "A" tasks before the "B" tasks and all of the "B" tasks before the "C" tasks.
- Carry over tasks that are not completed from the previous day to the next day's list.

An example of a task list is provided here. See if you like this format for your task list.

Sample Task List

Priority Rating	Task	Date Put on List	Date Completed
A			
A			
.			
.			
B			
.			
.			
.			
.			
.			
.			
C			
.			
.			
.			
.			
.			
.			

Note: This format can be used for a paper system. Many electronic systems allow you to assign priority ratings as well. You should use the system that best fits your needs.

CHAPTER 6: Problem Solving and Managing Overwhelming Tasks

OVERVIEW

The main skills that you will learn in this chapter are how to solve problems effectively and how to take a task that, at first, seems overwhelming and break it down into manageable steps. The problem-solving techniques are adapted from cognitive-behavioral interventions that focus exclusively on problem solving (i.e., D'Zurilla, 1986; Nezu, Nezu, Friedman, Faddis, & Houts, 1998).

GOALS

- To continue to monitor your progress
- To review your use of the calendar and task list, particularly the "A," "B," "C" priority ratings
- To learn how to use problem-solving techniques to overcome difficulties with task completion or selection of a solution
- To learn how to break a large task into manageable steps
- To troubleshoot difficulties with breaking down large tasks into manageable steps
- To identify exercises for home practice

Review of Symptom Checklist

As you have been doing each week, complete the ASRS Symptom Checklist at the start of your therapy session, and share this information with your therapist.

Score: _____   Date: _____

Review of Medication Adherence

As you have been doing each week, record your prescribed dosage of medication and indicate the number of doses you missed. Review triggers for missed doses such as distractibility, running out of medication, or thoughts about not wanting/needing to take medication.

Prescribed doses per week: _____

Doses missed this week: _____

Triggers for missed doses:

_____

_____

Review of Previous Chapters

Each week you should examine your progress in implementing the skills you have learned so far in this treatment. It is important to acknowledge the successes you have achieved and try to resolve any difficulties.

To review, the tools for organization and planning are as follows:

- Use of calendar for managing appointments
- Use of task list system
- Use of the "A," "B," and "C" priority ratings

Skill: Problem-Solving Strategies

This section involves learning to recognize when you are having difficulty completing a task or are becoming overwhelmed and cannot figure out exactly where to start. The reason we call problems "problems" is because there is no easy solution at hand. Usually any solution has serious pros and cons, and this typically can lead to problems like procrastination.

Once you recognize that there is a problem, you can use these problem-solving strategies to help. We are going to go over two skills that may seem simple but are actually quite powerful: (1) selecting an action plan and (2) breaking down an overwhelming task into manageable steps.

Developing an action plan can be helpful when it is difficult to determine how to resolve a problem or when the possibility of numerous solutions becomes overwhelming. Selecting an action plan involves the five steps in problem solving that are listed below.

Skill: Five Steps in Problem Solving

Use these instructions in conjunction with the sheet on page 112.

1. **Articulate the problem**: Try to describe the problem in as few words as possible—one or two sentences at the most. Examples might be "I cannot decide whether I should quit my job" or "I cannot decide what color to paint my house."
2. **List all possible solutions**: In this column, you want to try to figure out all of the different solutions—regardless of how realistic they are, what the consequences may be, or whether or not they sound outrageous. The idea is to generate a list of as many solutions as possible.
3. **List the pros and cons of each solution**: Now is the time to realistically appraise each solution. In these columns you want to figure out what you think would happen if you picked that solution. List the pros (advantages) and cons (disadvantages) of each.
4. **Rate each solution**: Using the final column, rate the pros and cons of the solution on a scale from 1 to 10, with 1 being a terrible solution and 10 being a great solution. Try to be as objective as possible, but include the relative difficulty it would take to carry out this solution. For example, if one solution is to assertively say "no" to something, you should factor in whether this will be anxiety provoking, as well as whether it will be likely to have the desired outcome.
5. **Implement the best option**: Now that you have rated each option on a scale of 1 to 10, review each rating. Look at the one that is rated the highest. Determine if this is really the solution that you would

like to pick. If so, use the other skills you have learned in this treatment program (problem solving, organizing, task list, calendar) to implement it.

Skill: Breaking Down Large Tasks into Manageable Steps

If a task seems overwhelming, we are much more likely to procrastinate and not even attempt to start working on the task. Even if the solution is clear, it may just feel easier to put off working on the overwhelming task. By learning how to break down large tasks into smaller, more manageable, steps, you will increase the likelihood that you will start (and therefore eventually complete) important tasks.

Here are the steps for breaking down large tasks into manageable steps:

1. **Choose a difficult or complex task from your task list** (or the solution that you identified as the best option on the problem-solving worksheet from the previous exercise).
2. **List the steps that you must complete.** You can do this using small notecards or plain paper or you can type the steps into your phone, tablet, or computer. Ask questions such as, "What is the first thing that I would need to do to make this happen?"
3. **For each step, make sure that it is manageable.** Ask yourself, "Is this something that I could realistically complete in one day?" and "Is this something that I would want to put off doing?" If the step itself is overwhelming, then break that step into smaller steps. Don't be afraid to have more steps.
4. **Add each individual step to the master list.**
5. **Individual steps can be moved to the daily task lists one at a time as needed**—just put the step or steps that you are hoping to complete on a particular day on the daily list for that day.
6. **Individual tasks can be placed on your calendar in specific time slots if you find this helpful.**

Potential Pitfalls

You may find that distractibility interferes with your ability to use these skills. Don't despair! You will learn skills for coping with distractibility in the next module. It is important to focus on one set of skills at a time so that you can make progress. Try to focus on applying the organizational skills as best you can and don't worry about the issues that you have not learned to deal with yet.

Also, you may find that you have some difficulty figuring out how to rate the pros, cons, and overall desirability of solutions and deciding how many steps make sense for each task. Remember, each new skill will take lots of practice before it comes naturally to you. The most important thing is that you are trying to learn new skills so that you can be more effective and organized. Just keep trying! It will get easier as you get used to using the new skills.

Practice

- Continue to put all appointments on the calendar.
- Put all tasks on the master task list.
- Use and look at the task list and calendar EVERY DAY!
- Rate each task as an "A," "B," or "C" task.
- Practice doing all of the "A" tasks before the "B" tasks and all of the "B" tasks before the "C" tasks.
- Carry over tasks that are not completed to the next day's daily task list.
- Practice using Worksheet 1: *Problem Solving: Selection of Action Plan* for at least one item on the task list. Worksheets are located in the Appendix at the end of this workbook.
- Practice breaking down one large task from the task list into smaller steps.

CHAPTER 7: Organizational Systems

OVERVIEW

The main goal of this chapter is for you to learn strategies for developing organizational systems. You can develop a system to use to deal with mail and incoming papers. You can also work on developing any other types of organizational systems that might be helpful for you, such as computer files, emails, or items in various areas of your home.

For the paper filing system, you will learn both how to "triage" (order the importance of and organize) papers as they come in and how to develop a filing system so that you can find important papers later when you need them. In addition, part of this session involves reviewing the organizational skills that you have learned so far in this module so that you will be ready to move on to the module on distractibility next week.

GOALS

- To continue to monitor your progress
- To review your use of the calendar and task list
- To review your use of the "A," "B," and "C" priority ratings
- To review your use of problem solving and breaking down large tasks into manageable steps
- To develop a sorting system for dealing with papers and mail
- To develop a filing system for important papers
- To develop other organizational systems that might be useful
- To identify exercises for home practice and anticipate difficulties using these techniques

Review of Symptom Checklist

As you have been doing each week, complete the ASRS Symptom Checklist at the start of your therapy session, and share this information with your therapist.

Score: _____   Date: _____

Review of Medication Adherence

As you have been doing each week, record your prescribed dosage of medication and indicate the number of doses you missed. List triggers for missed doses.

Prescribed doses per week: _____

Doses missed this week: _____

Triggers for missed doses:

_____

_____

Review of Previous Chapters

Each week you should examine your progress in implementing the skills that you have learned so far in this treatment. It is important to acknowledge the successes you have achieved and to try to resolve any difficulties.

To review, the tools for organization and planning are as follows:

- Use of calendar for managing appointments: Discuss any problems you are having with using your calendar system.
- Use of task list system: Review any difficulties you are having with using your task list on a daily basis.
- Use of the "A," "B," and "C" priority ratings: Discuss any trouble you are having with prioritizing tasks.
- Use of problem solving (selecting an action plan) and breaking down large tasks into small steps: Consider your use of these strategies and practice one or both skills using examples from your current task list.

Skill: Developing a Sorting System for Mail

Most people find it somewhat difficult to organize mail, important papers, and bills. Now that so many things are delivered electronically, this problem can apply to emails and electronic files as well as to actual papers. Individuals with ADHD can find it overwhelming to deal with these issues. This can lead to getting into arguments with people you live with, not paying bills on time, and misplacing important documents.

Putting a structured system in place can make this issue feel less overwhelming and more manageable. In this session, you will be learning about organizational strategies. Using these strategies may feel unfamiliar and may take some additional time to implement in the **short term**, but in the **long term**, these strategies will make organization much easier.

When you have an organizational system in place, it will decrease difficulties related to poor organization such as feeling overwhelmed or out of control, paying late fees, and missing out on opportunities because of missed deadlines or lost paperwork.

We recommend involving your spouse, partner, or roommate in helping to come up with a system that is mutually agreeable. Worksheet 2: *Steps for Sorting Mail* (in the Appendix) lists some proposed steps.

Paying Bills

One big concern that we frequently hear about from individuals with ADHD is that they do not want to pay bills until near the time they are due. Some people feel that this will save money because if they do this for all of their bills, they will get more interest on the money in the bank. Other people feel that they want to wait because they want to have their money longer, while others just simply procrastinate around paying bills. Typically, what happens is that people who delay paying their bills end up paying them late, incurring fees, and losing money.

The best time to deal with bills and other household task list items is right away. Look at your bills and other action items two or three times a week so that there are not many things you need to deal with at any given time and it will be less overwhelming. However, sometimes it is just as easy to pay the bill right away as it is to file it for later payment. Using the OHIO (Only Handle It Once) technique can save you lots of time, money, and aggravation. Since so many bills and other important communications are delivered electronically now, apply this strategy to your email as well as to your paper mail. You can develop a strategy for "flagging" items in your email that need attention or you can save them to a special folder.

Automatic Payments

You may want to consider setting up automatic payments for bills that you need to pay on a regular basis. Payments such as mortgage or rent payments, car payments, and student loan payments are typically due on the same day each month and are a consistent dollar amount. You can set up a payment with your bank so that a check or electronic payment will be sent out automatically each month. For other bills, such as credit card bills, that have different amounts due each month, you can set up an automatic payment to ensure that at least the minimum payment gets sent in each month (so you will not incur late charges or damage your credit score). You can then set up reminders for yourself to make additional payments during the month.

You will need to put a system in place for checking your bank account periodically to make sure that there is enough money in your account to cover all of the automatic payments that you have set up. You may want to integrate this into your calendar system (e.g., make a reminder to check your bank balance just before large automatic payments are due each month). In addition, most banks will allow you to set up alerts that will text message or email you when the balance falls below a certain threshold so that you can add funds.

Even with automatic payments in place, it is likely that there will be occasions when bills come in that fall outside of the payment system. For example, medical bills, utility bills (e.g., water bill), parking violations, tax bills, and so on may not easily lend themselves to the automatic payment system. You should have a way of dealing with these types of bills so that they don't "fall through the cracks." Perhaps you could write them down on your task list and cross them off when they have been paid, or you could put the email reminders in a folder and delete them once you have paid the bill.

Skill: Developing an Organizational System

Another common struggle for people with ADHD is keeping papers, electronic files, and other items organized. Without systems in place, people lose items, leading to frustration when they need these articles, or miss deadlines because they can't find important information. Furthermore, many people find it difficult to throw things away, resulting in a cluttered environment, which makes it even more difficult to find important papers or other items. We recommend coming up with organizational systems that are both simple and effective. If systems are too complicated, they are time consuming to use and people stop using them.

Before coming up with systems, assess where you are having difficulties with organization—for example, email, paperwork, computer files, or areas of your home are common difficulties. You can think about difficulties that may be caused by the organizational problems. If you are in a relationship, these issues can often cause relationship difficulties. As noted above, disorganization can lead to financial difficulties in the form of wasted money on late payment fees, poor credit scores, and so on. It is helpful to start off with an area that is really upsetting for you. Look at Worksheet 3: *Developing an Organizational System* (in the Appendix) to help you come up with your own system.

Potential Pitfalls

One potential pitfall is thinking that everything is important. This is just not true. Discuss with people who are close to you what items or files really need to be saved, and come up with a firm list.

It may take some time in the short term to set up these systems, but it will be worth it in the long term! Try to use the strategies of problem solving and breaking down large tasks into smaller steps if you feel overwhelmed by the prospect of setting up your organizational systems. If you take one step at a time, you will be able to complete these tasks.

You may need to discuss your proposed systems with other family members before you set them up. It will work much better if everyone is "on the same page" about where everything goes. For example, if your spouse is still putting the mail in a big pile on the chair and you are trying to put the important items in a special bin on the kitchen counter, it won't work very well.

Practice

- Continue to use the calendar every day to record appointments, and put new tasks on the task list every day.
- Use and look at the task list and calendar EVERY DAY!
- Rate each task as an "A," "B," or "C" task.
- Practice doing all of the "A" tasks before the "B" tasks and all of the "B" tasks before the "C" tasks.
- Carry over tasks that are not completed to the next day's task list.
- Practice using Worksheet 1: *Problem Solving: Selection of Action Plan* for at least one item on the task list.
- Practice breaking down one large task from the task list into smaller steps.
- Set up and use the organizational systems developed in session.

MODULE 2

Reducing Distractibility

CHAPTER 8: Gauging Your Attention Span and Distractibility Delay

OVERVIEW

The main goals of this chapter are for you to (1) figure out how long you can hold your attention when doing "dreaded" tasks and (2) start implementing the "distractibility delay." The distractibility delay involves timing your ability to stay focused on difficult activities, and also reducing tasks into "chunks" that take approximately that length of time. You will also learn how to delay the time when you become distracted from the task at hand.

GOALS

- To continue to monitor your progress
- To review your use of the calendar, task list, and work from previous chapters
- To learn how to gauge your attention span and develop a plan for breaking tasks down into steps that take that length of time
- To implement the distractibility delay
- To identify exercises for home practice and anticipate difficulties using these techniques

Review of Symptom Checklist

As you have been doing each week, complete the ASRS Symptom Checklist at the start of your therapy session, and share this information with your therapist.

Score: _____   Date: _____

Review of Medication Adherence

As you have been doing each week, record your prescribed dosage of medication and indicate the number of doses you missed. List triggers for missed doses.

Prescribed Doses/ per week: _____

Doses missed this week: _____

Triggers for missed doses:

_____

_____

Review of Previous Chapters

Each week you should review your progress implementing skills from each of the previous chapters. It is important to acknowledge the successes you have achieved and to try to resolve any difficulties.

To review, here are the tools for organization and planning:

- Use of calendar for managing appointments: Discuss any problems you are having with using your calendar system.
- Use of task list system: Review any difficulties you are having with using your task list on a daily basis.
- Use of the "A," "B," and "C" priority ratings: Discuss any trouble you are having with prioritizing tasks.
- Use of problem solving (selecting an action plan) and breaking down large tasks into small steps: Consider your use of these strategies, and practice one or both skills using examples from your current task list.

Concepts of Attention Span and Distractibility

Commonly clients with ADHD report that they are unable to complete tasks because other, less important tasks or distractions get in the way. Having a short attention span is part of ADHD. We do not view having a low attention span as being associated with low intelligence or lack of ability, but rather as representing a need for people with ADHD to use extra skills in order to cope.

There are many examples of people who can do extraordinary things despite having certain limitations. An extreme example is the musician Stevie Wonder. Even though he is blind, he used extra coping skills to become a top recording star.

The goal of treatment is to help you function at an optimal level. We will use several strategies to help you accomplish this goal.

Skill: Gauging Your Attention Span

There really is no such thing as an exact amount of time representing each individual's attention span. The amount of time that you can work on a particular task will depend on many factors, including those related to the task (level of complexity) and those related to the individual (how tired you are, your level of interest in the task, whether you have eaten recently, and so on). What you are trying to gauge with the following exercise is a reasonable amount of time that you can expect yourself to work on a boring task. Often, individuals with ADHD will set unrealistic goals for themselves (e.g., "I am going to study for eight hours straight"), and then they end up not wanting to start the task because the goal is so overwhelming.

1. The first step is to estimate the length of time that you can work on a boring or unattractive task without stopping.
2. The second step is to use the problem-solving skills that you learned earlier to break down a task into steps that last this length of time. For example, if you think that you can work on a boring task for 10 minutes, break down a larger task (e.g., paying bills) into 10-minute chunks.

During the upcoming week, pick a task you know you have been avoiding. Find a way to time yourself while working on the task, using either a watch or the stopwatch function on your computer or smartphone.

- Figure out a time when you can work on a task that you may find boring or difficult or that you have been avoiding.
- Start timing yourself.
- Begin working.
- Keep going as long as you normally would before taking a break, or going to the bathroom, or having a strong distraction pop into your head.
- When the urge comes to stop working, record the time.

Repeat the above exercise a couple of times. Average out the amount of time that it took before you became distracted. This will be your starting attention span time.

Now the trick is to use the problem-solving skills you learned above to break down overwhelming or boring tasks into chunks that take approximately the amount of time that you can hold your attention. We recommend taking breaks only in between the chunks.

As you do this more and more, you can try to increase the length of time that you are able to focus on boring or unattractive tasks.

It is important not only to schedule specific times to work, but also to schedule in breaks. You should time both the work time blocks and the breaks so that you don't end up taking breaks that are too long. For example, it will take a long time to finish a task if you work for 30 minutes and then take a three-hour break.

Skill: Distractibility Delay

When you are working on a boring task, it is inevitable that distractions will "pop into your head" from time to time and serve as big temptations! Many times the distractions seem to grow in importance as time goes on.

The difficult problem here is figuring out whether these distractions are actually important OR whether they just become more important because (1) they are not the task you had set out to do now or (2) the task you set out to do now is not attractive.

Is It Important or Just More Attractive?

For example, one of our clients was working on his master's thesis. He told us that whenever he sat down to do his work, he would feel the need to clean his apartment. He did not like cleaning, but he would have the urge to clean whenever he needed to write. In fact, he got to the point where he felt that he just could not work unless everything in his apartment was cleaned and in order! Over the years, we have found that other clients who were in school would report similar stories. We now believe that the cleanest apartments in the world belong to graduate students who need to do their theses! In these cases, cleaning becomes a distraction that grows in importance. Even though it is typically not an attractive or important task, it becomes much more attractive than the task at hand, which feels overwhelming.

Once you have determined the length of time for which you can hold your attention, and you have broken down tasks into steps that take about that amount of time, the next step is to try to build skills in delaying distractions.

Distractibility Delay

The distractibility delay is an exercise that can be done in addition to the strategies described above. It is similar to an exercise used in anxiety-disorder treatments (e.g., Craske & Barlow, 2006) and can be used as a strategy for delaying attending to distractions while working on boring or unattractive tasks. Clients with ADHD often report that it is difficult when a thought pops into their head while they are working on a task. They say that it is tempting to simply stop working on their current task and shift to working on the new task. They report that this is because they worry about forgetting the new task and not completing it at all. The reality is that this has been the client's experience in the past. Thus, the distractibility delay can be described as a tool for getting the distractions out of your head and getting you to focus on the task at hand. Over time, you will gain confidence that these thoughts will not be forgotten and will actually get done.

When you start working on a boring or unattractive task, have a piece of paper or a note app open in your smartphone or other device. Set a timer (you can use your smartphone for this as well) for the agreed-upon length of time (e.g., 30 minutes). When a distraction comes into your head, write it down, but don't take action at that time. Instead, return to the task at hand. When the timer goes off, you can look at the list and decide if any of the distracting tasks need to be completed at that time.

Repeat this process until the task is completed (or the portion of the task that you have set out to do for the day). Then review the list of distractions and decide if (1) they need to be completed at that time, (2) they should be added to your master or daily task list, or (3) they are unimportant and do not need to be completed. Discard the piece of paper (or delete the electronic note) at the end of the exercise so that you don't end up with multiple lists.

You can use coping statements to help you return to the task at hand. These can include, "I will worry about this later," "This is not an A-priority task," or "I will come back to this."

You can use the distractibility delay in a similar fashion during meetings. For example, if you have difficulties with impulsively blurting out comments or questions, bring a notepad or tablet to meetings, write down a cue word or phrase, and then try to refocus your attention on the meeting. When there is a break in the conversation or after the meeting, you can bring up your question or comment.

Steps for Distractibility Delay

1. Next to you, put a piece of scrap paper or your phone with a blank, open "note."
2. Set your timer for a goal length of time—this should be the length of time for which you can usually hold your attention.
3. Start working on the task.
4. When a distraction pops into your head, write it down on your scrap paper or on your electronic note, but *don't do anything about it* (e.g., don't get up and start making a phone call, putting something away, writing a check, and so on).
5. Once you have written down the distraction, you can use coping statements such as, "I will worry about it later," "This is not an A-priority task," or "I will come back to this."
6. Return to the original task until you are finished with the "chunk" that you have selected.
7. When the timer goes off, take a break. At this point, you can look at your distraction list and decide if you want to do these tasks now or if you want to do them later.

8. When you are finished working for the day, go back to the distraction list. Decide if these are actually important or if they are things that became attractive only because they were not the task you were working on.
9. If they are in fact important, either do them or add them to your task list.

Potential Pitfalls

These skills may seem simple, but they aren't! Don't expect yourself to be able to use them effectively right away. The extra coping skills that you are learning to help you overcome your short attention span and distractibility may take some time to develop. Remember, it took you many years to develop your current habits, and it will take some time to develop the more effective habits. Stick with this program; it will be worth it in the long run!

Practice

- Continue to use the calendar every day to record appointments, and put new tasks on the task list every day.
- Use and look at the task list and calendar EVERY DAY!
- Rate each task as an "A," "B," or "C" task.
- Practice doing all of the "A" tasks before the "B" tasks and all of the "B" tasks before the "C" tasks.
- Carry over tasks that are not completed to the next day's task list.
- Practice using Worksheet 1: *Problem Solving: Selection of Action Plan* for at least one item on the task list.
- Practice breaking down one large task from the task list into smaller steps.
- Use the organizational systems developed in this program.
- Gauge your attention span.
- Use the distractibility delay when working on boring or unattractive tasks.

CHAPTER 9: Modifying Your Environment

OVERVIEW

The main goals of this chapter are for you to learn how to (1) modify your environment to reduce distractibility and (2) create reminders for yourself to focus on the task at hand.

You will learn how to reduce the number of distractions in your environment and create a situation that is more conducive to concentration. You will also learn a strategy that will help you check in with yourself to see if you are distracted. This will enable you to refocus your attention on the task at hand if you have become distracted.

GOALS

- To continue to monitor your progress
- To review your continued use of skills from previous chapters
- To continue breaking tasks down into steps that match your attention span, and using the distractibility delay
- To learn how to reduce the number of things that are likely to distract you in your environment
- To learn how to check in with yourself to see if you are distracted and learn how to refocus on the task at hand when you do become distracted
- To identify exercises for home practice and anticipate difficulties using these techniques

Review of Symptom Checklist

As you have been doing each week, complete the ASRS Symptom Checklist at the start of your therapy session, and share this information with your therapist.

Score: _____   Date: _____

Review of Medication Adherence

As you have been doing each week, record your prescribed dosage of medication and indicate the number of doses you missed. List triggers for missed doses.

Prescribed doses per week: _____

Doses missed this week: _____

Triggers for missed doses:

_____

_____

Review of Previous Chapters

Each week you should review your progress implementing skills from each of the previous chapters. It is important to acknowledge the successes you have achieved and try to resolve any difficulties.

To review, here are the tools for organization and planning:

- Use of calendar for managing appointments: Discuss any problems you are having with using your calendar system.
- Use of task list system: Review any difficulties you are having with using your task list on a daily basis.
- Use of the "A," "B," and "C" priority ratings: Discuss any trouble you are having with prioritizing tasks.
- Use of problem solving (selecting an action plan) and breaking down large tasks into small steps: Consider your use of these strategies and practice one or both skills using examples from your current task list.

Here are the tools for reducing distractibility:

- Use of the strategy of breaking tasks down into manageable chunks: Discuss any problems you are having with breaking down tasks.
- Use of the distractibility delay: Review any difficulties you are having with the distractibility delay technique.

Skill: Controlling Your Work Environment

It is important for individuals with ADHD to work in an environment that has few distractions. Even with the distractibility coping skills discussed above, most people are somewhat distractible when they are trying to concentrate. Sometimes, distractions interfere to the point where it is too difficult to get things done.

At this time, think about the environment in which you try to do work, schoolwork, or important household tasks (e.g., pay bills). Ask yourself, "What are the things that typically distract me from my work?" Some typical distractions include the following:

- The telephone ringing or a notification popping up on your phone, computer, or tablet
- Surfing the Internet, chatting online, playing online games, using social media
- Replying to emails or texts
- Noticing other things on the desk or table that need attention
- Listening to something on the radio
- Watching something on television
- Speaking to a friend or relative who is in the room
- Looking at something going on outside the window

What are the types of things that typically get in the way when you are trying to get a project done? For each item that is distracting to you, come up with a strategy that reduces your susceptibility to this distraction. For example, you can do the following:

- Silence your phone or put it on vibrate.
- Close your web browser and/or email.
- Turn off notifications on your phone, computer, or tablet.
- Clear off your desk or workspace.

- Turn off the radio and television.
- Ask others not to disturb you because you are working.
- Turn your desk away from the window.

Use Worksheet 4: *Strategies for Reducing Distractions* (in the Appendix) to identify and eliminate usual distractions for your work environment.

We recommend finding one place in your home where you can do important tasks without distractions. This place should be somewhere you are able to keep clear. It could be your desk, it could be a table near your desk, or it could be any other "workspace." Many people report that their desk becomes cluttered and is difficult to keep clean. Of course, you can use your organizational systems discussed above. However, if you think that having a messy desk may not change, the idea here is to find another space that you can use that you would keep clear, and have this be your workspace. You want to set the stage for success—by setting up a work environment that is conducive for you to be as productive as possible.

Interestingly, some people with ADHD report that they do not concentrate as well when they are in a totally silent environment. It may be helpful for you to try to articulate the circumstances that are the most helpful in aiding your ability to concentrate. For example, many clients report that they concentrate better when there is a certain type of music playing in the background (often classical music or other music that does not have lyrics that might be distracting).

Skill: Keeping Track of Important Objects

One hallmark of ADHD is that people with this disorder frequently lose important items. This is problematic because it can cause lateness and increase feelings of frustration.

At this point, take a moment to think of any difficulties that you experience with keeping track of important objects, such as your keys, wallet, or phone. Some of these may be items that you need to take with you whenever you leave the house.

The next step is to think of a specific place where you would like to keep these items. Some people will place a basket somewhere near the door and put the important items in the basket each time that they come in the door. Other people will have a hanging rack for all keys. You may be able to place all of your important items in one place, or you may need to come up with several different places.

Having specific places where the important items belong increases the likelihood that you will be able to locate the items when you need them. You need to work to develop the habit.

> **The goal is to try to never put down your keys or any of the other important items in any location except for its target location!**

You can improve the success of this technique by involving other family members in the process. You can tell everyone in the household where things belong, and ask them to either put the items away or to remind you to do so if they notice that something is out of place. (Of course, you have to agree not to get mad at them when they remind you!)

> **The other important (and many times difficult) task to do is this: Whenever you see one of these items out of place, you MUST immediately return it to the specified spot.**

Skill: Using Reminders

Imagine that you could have someone follow you around and constantly remind you about all of the skills that we have discussed. Having this person around would greatly increase your use of the skills. You would never forget. These skills require that you actively remember to do them. (With practice, though, these skills become habits and eventually you won't have to actively remember to use them.)

For most people, a 24-hour personal assistant is not feasible, so we recommend the use of reminders.

An alarm can be helpful in getting you to check in with yourself on a regular basis about whether or not you are on task. You can use an alarm clock, or an alarm on your watch, computer, or cellphone.

Set the alarm to go off at regularly scheduled intervals during time periods when you are trying to concentrate on a task. We recommend trying to have the alarm sound each half-hour—especially when you are trying to be productive.

When the alarm sounds, ask yourself, "Am I doing what I am supposed to be doing or did I get distracted?" If you notice that you have become distracted, immediately return to the task at hand.

Potential Pitfalls

It is easy to get frustrated with these strategies if they don't work right away. Remember, you are trying to develop new work habits. It takes lots of practice before new habits become second nature. Don't give up! Even if it seems like these skills don't work at first, keep at them. It will pay off in the long run when you are able to be less susceptible to distractions and get more accomplished.

Practice

- Continue to use the calendar every day to record appointments and put new tasks on the task list every day.
- Use and look at the task list and calendar EVERY DAY!
- Rate each task as an "A," "B," or "C" task.
- Practice doing all of the "A" tasks before the "B" tasks and all of the "B" tasks before the "C" tasks.
- Carry over tasks that are not completed to the next day's task list.
- Practice using Worksheet 1: *Problem Solving: Selection of Action Plan* for at least one item on the task list.
- Practice breaking down one large task from the task list into smaller steps.
- Use the organizational systems developed in this program.
- Use the distractibility delay when working on boring or unattractive tasks.
- Use your skills to reduce distraction in your work environment.
- Start putting important items in specific places.
- Use reminders to check in with yourself to see if you have become distracted when you are trying to focus on completing a task.

MODULE 3

Adaptive Thinking

CHAPTER 10: Introducing a Cognitive Model of ADHD

OVERVIEW

By now, you have developed systems for organizing, planning, and problem solving and have been practicing skills for managing distractibility. The next section, targeting adaptive thinking, will help you increase your awareness of negative thoughts that can cause stress and mood problems and that can interfere with the successful completion of tasks.

This method of training yourself to think adaptively has been used in similar cognitive-behavioral treatments and has been effective in treating many other psychological disorders, such as depression and anxiety disorders.[1] The major goal of learning to think about tasks and situations adaptively is to reduce the times when negative or ineffective thoughts or moods interfere with tasks, follow-through, or distress or add to distractibility.

Adaptive thinking will enable you to do the following:

- Increase your awareness of negative, interfering thoughts
- Develop strategies for keeping your thoughts in check
- Minimize symptoms

---

[1] This method of implementing and teaching cognitive-restructuring skills is based on McDermott (2000), as well as other cognitive-behavioral therapy manuals, including Hope and colleagues' 2000 manual for the treatment of social phobia, and the 1996 manual by Otto, Jones, Craske, and Barlow for the treatment of panic disorder in the context of medication discontinuation.

GOALS

- To continue to monitor your progress
- To review your continued use of skills from previous chapters
- To learn basic principles of the cognitive-behavioral model of mood
- To become skilled in identifying and labeling unhelpful automatic thoughts
- To identify exercises for home practice and anticipate difficulties using these techniques

Review of Symptom Checklist

As you have been doing each week, complete the ASRS Symptom Checklist at the start of your therapy session, and share this information with your therapist.

Score: _____   Date: _____

Review of Medication Adherence

As you have been doing each week, record your prescribed dosage of medication and indicate the number of doses you missed. List triggers for missed doses.

Prescribed doses per week: _____

Doses missed this week: _____

Triggers for missed doses:

_____

_____

Review of Previous Chapters

Each week you should review your progress implementing skills from each of the previous chapters It is important to acknowledge the successes you have achieved and to try to resolve any difficulties.

To review, here are the tools for organization and planning:

- Use of calendar for managing appointments: Discuss any problems you are having with using your calendar system.
- Use of task list system: Review any difficulties you are having with using your task list on a daily basis.
- Use of the "A," "B," and "C" priority ratings: Discuss any trouble you are having with prioritizing tasks.
- Use of problem solving (selecting an action plan) and breaking down large tasks into small steps: Consider your use of these strategies and practice one or both skills using examples from your current task list.

Here are the tools for reducing distractibility:

- Use of the strategy of breaking tasks down into manageable chunks: Discuss any problems you are having with breaking down tasks.
- Use of the distractibility delay: Review any difficulties you are having with the distractibility delay technique.
- Removing distractions from environment
- Identifying specific places for important items and making sure that the items always get put away in these places
- Use of reminders, "Am I doing what I am supposed to be doing?"

The Cognitive-Behavioral Model

Adaptive thinking is just what it sounds like: It is a way of thinking about situations in a manner that is adaptive or effective. Sometimes individuals have thoughts that are either inaccurate or unhelpful, and this can cause difficulties. By learning adaptive thinking, you can learn to challenge your inaccurate or unhelpful thoughts and come up with more effective ways of looking at situations. Adaptive thinking is important because of the interrelationship between thoughts, feelings, and behaviors (Fig. 10.1).

This model emphasizes the important connection between your thoughts, feelings, and behaviors in a given situation. The cognitive part of cognitive-behavioral therapy involves the manner in which thoughts contribute to how people act, and the way that thoughts contribute to how people feel.

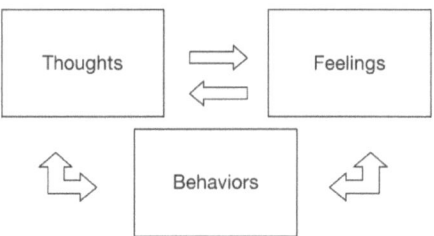

Figure 10.1

The cognitive-behavioral model

The Cognitive Component of Treatment: Automatic Thinking

Every day, numerous thoughts go through our minds. What is surprising is that often we are not particularly aware of these thoughts. However, they play an important role in determining how we are feeling in a situation, and how we may respond. When we are feeling overwhelmed or stressed or are anticipating completing a task, the thoughts that go through our minds play a critical role in determining the outcome of our situations.

These thoughts are "automatic"—they happen on their own. For example, think about when you first learned to drive a car. In order to coordinate many tasks at once, you had to be conscious of handling the steering wheel, remembering to signal for turns, staying exactly in your lane, avoiding other traffic, and trying to park. You were doing many tasks at the same time that required your total attention.

Now, think about driving today. You probably know how to drive without actively thinking about what you are doing. You likely don't even remember thinking about all of these steps because they have become automatic.

In many situations, like the one we describe above, automatic thoughts enable us to complete a task more easily. Unfortunately, in other situations, automatic thoughts interfere with achieving goals. For example, imagine you have to do a task you will probably not enjoy, such as preparing your tax return. Imagine the following types of thoughts going through your mind:

"I am careless and am going to do this wrong."
"This is going to take forever."

"If I complete my return, I will realize I owe money."
"If I owe money, I won't have enough for rent."

If these thoughts are going through your head, then you can easily see that this task will feel overwhelming and stressful. This will increase the chances that you will procrastinate by doing any other possible task.

Relationship of Thoughts to Feelings and Behaviors

The behavioral component here is usually some form of avoidance. Negative thoughts about a situation can make you avoid the situation because you (1) feel worse and (2) expect the outcome of the situation to be negative. Avoidance can lead to more anxiety, restlessness, and perhaps irritability or depression—the task doesn't get done, and then your feel even worse about it.

Anxiety and depression may lead to more negative thinking, and around and around the cycle goes, making the problem worse and worse. For people with ADHD, this cycle worsens other symptoms such as inattention, procrastination, frustration, and depression.

The first step in breaking this cycle is to identify and slow down negative or ineffective automatic thinking. Becoming more aware of situations when this occurs is the first step in learning to think in more adaptive ways.

Thinking That Is Too Positive

So far, we have talked about NEGATIVE automatic thoughts. However, researchers are now identifying another problematic way of thinking in adults with ADHD that involves overly optimistic thinking (Knouse & Mitchell, 2015). These authors claim that adults with ADHD often set overly optimistic goals and verbalize overly positive thoughts. This pattern can cause difficulties in that individuals feel good in the moment (e.g., "I don't really need to do this today because I have plenty of time to do it next weekend"). However, this causes problems when the thinking and goal setting are unrealistic and the person ends up failing to meet his or her goals. Thus, we will be working to identify both negative and overly positive thoughts.

Skill: Identifying Negative/Unhelpful Automatic Thoughts

The thought record is a tool that was developed to help you learn how to identify, slow down, and restructure negative and/or unhelpful automatic thoughts. You can use the thought records provided, or you can write down this information in your phone, on your computer, or on your tablet. There are several apps and websites that allow you to enter this information, if you prefer.

Let's start with a distressing situation that you experienced in the past week. Think about the past week and see if you can identify a time when you felt overwhelmed, stressed, sad, or upset.

Learning to completing a thought record is best done with the aid of your therapist, and takes a good amount of time to learn how to do (Figs. 10.2 and 10.3). We recommend practicing it over several sessions.

Column 1 should contain a brief description of the **situation**. When did it take place, where were you, with whom, what was going on, and so on? Ideally, the description of the situation would just be a sentence or two at most.

Column 2 should contain your **thoughts**—what was going through your mind at the time. What were you saying to yourself about the situation, about other people, and about your role in the situation? What were you afraid might happen? What is the worst thing that could happen if this feared outcome occurred? What does this mean about how the other person feels/thinks about you?

Time and Situation	Automatic Thoughts	Mood and Intensity
At home, thinking about doing my taxes	This is going to be so much work.	Overwhelmed (80)
	I am never going to finish it.	
	I am never going to find everything I need to.	Anxious (75)
	I am going to get audited.	Frustrated (80)
	I am going to end up having to pay so much money.	

Figure 10.2

Sample completed *3-Column Thought Record*

Time and Situation	Automatic Thoughts	Mood and Intensity

Figure 10.3

3-Column Thought Record for you to complete

When coming up with automatic thoughts, it is important to separate thoughts from feelings. Thoughts are what you think of the situation. Feelings go in the next column.

Column 3 should be a list of the **moods** or emotions you experienced. You may list several different feelings, and then rate the **intensity** of each feeling on a scale of 0 to 100 (0 = the least intense, 100 = the most intense). Examples of moods include angry, upset, happy, sad, depressed, anxious, and surprised.

Introduction to Thinking Errors

Now that you see how certain situations can trigger automatic thoughts and subsequent negative (or at times positive) feelings, let's look more closely at the nature of these automatic thoughts. In our experience, and in the work of other cognitive-behavioral therapists, common types of negative automatic thoughts often emerge. Moreover, you can begin to see how these types of thoughts may interfere with your ability to complete tasks and also contribute to feeling depressed, anxious, or frustrated.

In Box 10.1 you will find a list of common thinking errors. Review each one to make sure you understand them all, and then begin to look for patterns and determine which types of error may be especially problematic for you.

Box 10.1 Common Thinking Errors

All-or-nothing thinking: You see things in black and white categories. For example, ALL aspects of a project need to be completed immediately, or if your performance falls short of perfect, you see it as a total failure.

Overgeneralization: You see a single negative event as a never-ending pattern.

Mental Filter: You pick out a single negative detail and dwell on it exclusively, overlooking other positive aspects of the situation.

Disqualifying the positive: You reject positive experiences by insisting they "don't count" for some reason or other. In this way, you can maintain a negative belief that is contradicted by your everyday experiences.

Jumping to Conclusions: You make a negative interpretation, even though there are no definite facts that convincingly support your conclusion.

Mind Reading: You arbitrarily conclude that someone is reacting negatively to you, and you don't bother to check this out.

Fortune Telling: You anticipate that things will turn out badly, and you feel that your prediction is a predetermined fact.

Magnification/Minimization: You exaggerate the importance of things (such as your mistake, or someone else's achievement), or you inappropriately shrink things until they appear tiny (your own desirable qualities or other people's imperfections).

Catastrophizing: You attribute extreme and horrible consequences to the outcomes of events. One mistake at work = being fired from your job.

Emotional Reasoning: You assume that your negative emotions necessarily reflect the way things really are: "I feel it, so it must be true."

"Should" Statements: You try to motivate yourself with "shoulds" and "shouldn'ts," as if you need to be punished before you could be expected to do anything. When directed toward others, you feel anger, frustration, and resentment.

Labeling and Mislabeling: This is an extreme form of overgeneralization. Instead of describing an error, you attach a negative label to yourself or others.

Personalization: You see negative events as indicative of some negative characteristic of yourself or others, or you take responsibility for events that were not your doing.

Maladaptive Thinking: You focus on a thought that may be true, but over which you have no control. Excessively thinking about it can be self-critical, or can distract you from an important task or from attempting new behaviors.

Overly Optimistic Thinking: You think about a situation in an overly optimistic way that feels good in the moment but leads to procrastination and/or avoidance and is not effective in the long-run.

This list is modified from Hope, Heimberg, Juster, and Turk (2000), which was in turn based on Persons (1989). Overly optimistic thinking is derived from Knouse and Mitchell (2015).

Skill: Labeling Thinking Errors

Now that you have learned about common types of thinking errors, let's go back to the thought record you filled out earlier. For each of the automatic thoughts you listed, review the list of thinking errors and see if you can identify these common patterns in your thinking. Then, list the appropriate thinking error in **Column 4.**

Keep in mind that not all negative thoughts represent thinking errors. Sometimes it is realistic that a situation produces a negative thought, which in turn contributes to a negative feeling. For example, imagine you had been studying for an exam for many days and you were driving to school to take the exam. Then, suddenly you encountered a traffic jam due to a car accident that occurred earlier. Now, if your thought was, "Oh no! I hope I won't be late! I studied so hard for this exam," and you were feeling anxious and perhaps frustrated, that would make sense! The challenge for you would be to *problem solve*—in other words, to try and stay calm, perhaps to call the instructor to let her know you are going to be late, and to focus on driving safely.

However, if in addition to those thoughts you also said to yourself, "Bad things always happen to me, I can never do anything right. I am going to miss the exam and fail the class," we can imagine that your anxiety and despair would intensify, and that you may be more likely to drive dangerously. Furthermore, if you did get to the exam in time, you most likely would not be able to concentrate as well as you did when you were studying. Looking closely, you can see that these thoughts, respectively, could be classified as *overgeneralization, personalization*, and *jumping to conclusions*. See the example in Figure 10.4, and then you can use the blank chart (Fig. 10.5) to record your own examples of negative and/or ineffective thoughts.

Time and Situation	Automatic Thoughts	Mood and Intensity	Thinking Error
Preparing a report for work	I have to do all of this today.	Overwhelmed (80)	All-or-nothing thinking
	I must do this perfectly.	Anxious (75)	All-or-nothing thinking
	If I do not finish my boss will be upset.	Depressed (60)	Jumping to conclusions (mind-reading)
	If the project is not perfect and my boss is upset, I will lose my job.		Jumping to conclusions (fortune-telling), Catastrophizing

Figure 10.4

Sample completed *4-Column Thought Record*

Time and Situation	Automatic Thoughts	Mood and Intensity	Thinking Error

Figure 10.5
4-Column Thought Record for you to complete

Potential Pitfalls

For some people, writing out negative thoughts makes the thoughts "seem more real" or more difficult to cope with. Because of this, they are reluctant to use thought records. However, the thought is in your mind, interfering, regardless of whether you write it down. Completing the thought record will actually help you feel better about the situation, despite the initial difficulty of seeing your thought written out on paper or electronically.

You may find that it is hard to label your feelings and may think that you have to come up with the perfect emotion to describe your feelings. In actuality, this is not true. Use the first word that comes to mind, even if it is not perfect. Over time, it will become easier to label your feelings.

Preliminary Instructions for Adaptive Thinking

The purpose of using thought records is to identify and modify negative, automatic thoughts in situations that lead to feeling overwhelmed.

The first step in learning to think in more useful ways is to become more aware of these thoughts and their relationship to your feelings. If you are anticipating a stressful situation, or a task that is making you feel overwhelmed, write out your thoughts regarding this situation.

If a situation has already passed and you find that you are thinking about it negatively or if, in retrospect, you realize that you were having unhelpful thoughts, list your thoughts for this situation.

The first column is a description of the situation.

The second column is for you to list your thoughts during a stressful, overwhelming, or uncontrollable situation.

The third column is for you to write down what emotions or feelings you are having when thinking these thoughts (e.g., depressed, sad, angry).

The fourth column is for you to see if your thoughts match the list of thinking errors. These may include the following:

- *All-or-Nothing Thinking*
- *Overgeneralizations*
- *Jumping to Conclusions (Fortune Telling/Mind Reading)*
- *Magnification/Minimization*
- *Emotional Reasoning*
- *"Should" Statements*
- *Labeling and Mislabeling*
- *Personalization*
- *Maladaptive Thinking*
- *Overly Optimistic Thinking*

Practice

> *In this session, try to anticipate which situations you may want to work on in the upcoming week. In addition, be sure to anticipate any problems that may get in the way of completing the practice exercises. For example, having a busy schedule, going out of town, or being uncertain about how to complete an assignment may make it more difficult to practice your skills. We have found that if you can anticipate and try to resolve any problems in advance, these obstacles can become manageable, and you will be more likely to achieve success with the new skills. Remember that you do not have to complete these home assignments perfectly! The idea is to begin monitoring your thoughts that arise in difficult situations and begin practicing identifying the common types of thinking errors.*

- Continue to use the calendar every day to record appointments and put new tasks on the task list every day.
- Use and look at the task list and calendar EVERY DAY!
- Rate each task as an "A," "B," or "C" task.
- Practice doing all of the "A" tasks before the "B" tasks and all of the "B" tasks before the "C" tasks.
- Carry over tasks that are not completed to the next day's task list.
- Practice using Worksheet 1: *Problem Solving: Selection of Action Plan* for at least one item on the task list.
- Practice breaking down one large task from the task list into smaller steps.
- Use the organizational systems developed in this program.
- Use the distractibility delay when working on boring or unattractive tasks.
- Use your skills to reduce distraction in your work environment.
- Start putting important items in specific places.
- Use reminders to check in with yourself to see if you have become distracted when you are trying to focus on completing a task.
- Read the "Preliminary Instructions for Adaptive Thinking" about completing a thought record.
- Complete thought records for at least two situations during the week.

As you have learned from the previous modules, practicing new skills is vital so that you become familiar with them, are able to easily use the tools, and begin to see the positive results that can emerge when you consistently use these cognitive-behavioral strategies. Recognize that, at first, when you are learning a new skill, it may feel awkward, may be confusing, and may require effort to implement. That's okay! The more you practice, the easier it will become.

CHAPTER 11: Adaptive Thinking

OVERVIEW

The primary goal of this chapter is for you to learn how to develop alternative thoughts to replace your negative and/or unhelpful thoughts. You will do this by working through a process called cognitive restructuring that involves observing your thoughts, labeling them as inaccurate or unhelpful, and then coming up with more accurate or helpful thoughts.

GOALS

- To continue to monitor your progress with the Symptom Checklist
- To review your continued use of skills from previous chapters
- To review thought records completed at home
- To discuss coaching styles and the coaching story
- To discuss formulation of a rational response
- To identify exercises for home practice

Review of Symptom Checklist

As you have been doing each week, complete the ASRS Symptom Checklist at the start of your therapy session, and share this information with your therapist.

Score: _____   Date: _____

Review of Medication Adherence

As you have been doing each week, record your prescribed dosage of medication and indicate the number of doses you missed. List triggers for missed doses.

Prescribed doses per week: _____

Doses missed this week: _____

Triggers for missed doses:

_____

_____

Review of Previous Chapters

Each week you should review your progress implementing skills from each of the previous chapters. It is important to acknowledge the successes you have achieved and to try to resolve any difficulties.

Here are the tools for organization and planning:

- Use of calendar for managing appointments: Discuss any problems you are having with using your calendar system.
- Use of task list system: Review any difficulties you are having with using your task list on a daily basis.
- Use of the "A," "B," and "C" priority ratings: Discuss any trouble you are having with prioritizing tasks.
- Use of problem solving (selecting an action plan) and breaking down large tasks into small steps: Consider your use of these strategies and practice one or both skills using examples from your current task list.

Here are the tools for reducing distractibility:

- Use of the strategy of breaking tasks down into manageable chunks: Discuss with your therapist any problems you are having with breaking down tasks.
- Use of the distractibility delay: Review any difficulties you are having with the distractibility delay technique.
- Removing distractions from environment

- Identifying specific places for important items and making sure that the items always get put away in these places
- Use of reminders, "Am I doing what I am supposed to be doing?"

Here are the tools for developing adaptive thinking:

- Use of thought records to identify and label automatic thoughts

Review the thought records you completed at home. If you were not able to complete any thought records, try to identify the obstacles that may have interfered, and use the problem-solving skills to determine the best way to work on automatic thinking. Did you have difficulty making time for home practice? Were the directions confusing? Was it difficult to see your thoughts in writing?

If you didn't do any thought records at home, it may be useful to practice doing one together with your therapist before going on.

If you did, then you should review for each situation the automatic thoughts and the thinking errors that you identified. Did you see any patterns?

Sometimes it can be tricky to sort out thoughts from feelings. Your therapist can help with this, and you can practice asking yourself, "Is this what I was *thinking* or *feeling*?"

Skill: Formulating a Rational Response

In this session, you will learn strategies to correct thinking errors and develop more helpful thoughts. Our goal is to help you transform the unhelpful, interfering thoughts into more supportive, helpful coaching thoughts. To understand how powerful your thoughts can be, we like to tell the coaching story in Box 11.1.

This story is meant to help you recognize negative, unhelpful thoughts as they pop up (Coach A thoughts) and to learn to develop more supportive, rational thinking (Coach B thoughts).

Let's go back to one of the thought records you previously completed. Review the automatic thoughts and thinking errors that you identified. If you have not completed a thought record yet, begin one now. The next step is to evaluate the helpfulness of each thought. The following

Box 11.1 Coaching Story

This is a story about Little League baseball. I talk about Little League baseball because of the amazing parents and coaches involved. And by "amazing" I don't mean good. I mean extreme. You will see how it relates to ADHD and how you talk to yourself.

But this story doesn't start with the coaches or the parents; it starts with Johnny, who is a Little League player in the outfield. His job is to catch "fly balls" and return them to the infield players. On this particular day of our story, Johnny is in the outfield. And "crack!"—one of the players on the other team hits a fly ball. The ball is coming to Johnny. Johnny raises his glove. The ball is coming to him, it is coming to him ... Johnny jumps up as high as he can, but he is in the wrong place at the wrong time doing the wrong strategy, so it goes over his head. Johnny misses the ball, and the other team scores a run.

Now there are a number of ways a coach can respond to this situation. Let's take Coach A first. Coach A is the type of coach who will come out on the field and shout, "I can't believe you missed that ball! Anyone could have caught it! My dog could have caught it! You screw up like that again and you'll be sitting on the bench! That was lousy!"

Coach A then storms off the field. At this point, if Johnny is anything like I am, he is standing there, tense, tight, trying not to cry, and praying that another ball is not hit to him. If a ball does come to him, Johnny will probably miss it. After all, he is tense tight, and may see four balls coming to him because of the tears in his eyes. Also, if we are Johnny's parents, we may see more profound changes after the game: Johnny, who typically places his baseball glove on the mantel, now throws it under his bed. And before the next game, he may complain that his stomach hurts, that perhaps he should not go to the game. This is the scenario with Coach A.

Now let's go back to the original event and play it differently. Johnny has just missed the fly ball, and now Coach B comes out on the field. Coach B says, "Well, you missed that one. Here is what I want you to remember: fly balls always look like they are farther away than they really are. Also, it is much easier to run forward than to back up. Because of this, I want you to prepare for the ball by taking a few extra steps backwards. Run forward if you need to, but try to catch it at chest level, so you can adjust your hand if you misjudge the ball. Let's see how you do next time."

Coach B leaves the field. How does Johnny feel? Well, he is not happy. After all, he missed the ball—but there are a number of important differences from the way he felt with Coach A. He is not as tense or tight, and if a fly ball does come to him, he knows what to do differently to catch it. And because he does not have tears in his eyes, he may actually see the ball accurately. He may catch the next one.

So, if we were the type of parent that eventually wants Johnny to make the Major League, we would pick Coach B, because he teaches Johnny how to be a more effective player. Johnny knows what to do differently, may catch more balls, and may excel at the game. But if we don't care whether Johnny makes the Major League—because baseball is a game, and one is supposed to be able to enjoy a game—then we would still pick Coach B. We pick Coach B because we care whether Johnny enjoys the game. With Coach B, Johnny knows what to do differently; he is not tight, tense, and ready to cry; he may catch a few balls; and he may enjoy the game. And he may continue to place his glove on the mantel.

Now, while we may all select Coach B for Johnny, we rarely choose the view of Coach B for the way we talk to ourselves. Think about your last mistake. Did you say, "I can't believe I did that! I am so stupid! What a jerk!"? These are "Coach A" thoughts and they have approximately the same effect on us as they do on Johnny. They make us feel tense and tight, and sometimes make us feel like crying. And this style of coaching rarely makes us do better in the future. Even if you are only concerned about productivity (making the Major League) you would still pick Coach B. And if you were concerned with enjoying life, while guiding yourself effectively for both joy and productivity, you would still pick Coach B.

Keep in mind that we are not talking about how we coach ourselves in a baseball game. We are talking about how we coach ourselves in life, and our enjoyment of life. People with excessive distress, and many with ADHD, tend to talk to themselves this way.

During the next week, I would like you to listen to see how you are coaching yourself. And if you hear Coach A, remember this story and see if you can replace Coach A with Coach B.

Reprinted from Otto, M. (2000). Stories and metaphors in cognitive-behavior therapy. *Cognitive and Behavioral Practice, 7*(2), 166–172. Copyright 2000, with permission from Elsevier.

Time and Situation	Automatic Thoughts	Mood and Intensity	Thinking Error	Rational Response
Preparing a report for work	I have to do all of this today.	Overwhelmed (80)	All-or-nothing thinking	I don't need to do it all today. I can get a start today and finish it up tomorrow.
	I must do this perfectly.	Anxious (75)	All-or-nothing thinking	
	If I do not finish my boss will be upset.	Depressed (60)	Jumping to conclusions (mind-reading)	I can ask my boss for help if I need it.
	If the project is not perfect and my boss is upset, I will lose my job.		Jumping to conclusions (fortune-telling), Catastrophizing	My boss has been really understanding in the past, so I don't think she will react any differently this time. I have worked at this company for over a year and gotten good feedback on many projects, so it is unlikely that I would lose my job if this project isn't perfect.

Figure 11.1

Sample completed *5-Column Thought Record*

questions are suggested prompts to help you objectively evaluate these thoughts:

- What is the evidence that this thought is true?
- Is there an alternative explanation?
- What is the worst thing that can happen?
- Has this situation unreasonably grown in importance?

- *What would a good coach say about this situation?*
- *Have I done what I can to control it?*
- *If I were to do anything else, would this help or hinder the situation?*
- *Am I worrying excessively about this?*
- *What would a good friend say to me about this situation?*
- *What would I say to a good friend about this situation if he or she were going through it?*
- *Why is this statement a thinking error?*

We now need to move to the *5-Column Thinking Record*, which is the final version of the thinking record that we will be using in this program (Figs. 11.1 and 11.2). In the last, and very important, column, you formulate a *rational response*. The rational response is a statement that you can say to yourself to try to feel better about the situation. Keep in mind that we are not asking you to overlook *all* negative aspects of your thoughts. Rather, the idea is to come up with a more balanced, objective, and helpful way of thinking about the situation.

Time and Situation	Automatic Thoughts	Mood and Intensity	Thinking Error	Rational Response

Figure 11.2

5-Column Thought Record

Remember that even if thoughts are true (e.g., "I didn't study as much as I would have liked for that test"), it may not be helpful to focus on them in a particular situation (e.g., as you are walking into the classroom to take the test in question). In that case, the strategy is not necessarily to argue with yourself about whether the thought is true, but simply to point out that it is unhelpful to focus on the thought at this time.

Potential Pitfalls

We have discussed several different types of thinking errors that can contribute to negative feelings and behaviors. While it is important to be familiar with the types of errors you may be making, don't get stuck trying to find the exact type of error that corresponds with your thought. Your thought may fit into more than one category, and often these categories of thinking errors overlap. Your goal is to recognize that your automatic thought might be a thinking error, to understand why this is true, and, most importantly, to come up with a rational response.

Identifying a rational response may be tricky at first. Refer to the suggested questions (e.g., *What would you say to a friend who said this?*). Also, keep in mind that your thoughts and feelings about the situation may not completely change immediately after identifying a rational response. However, if you repeat the more helpful responses to yourself, they will begin to replace the negative, automatic thoughts you initially had.

Instructions for Completing the *5-Column Thought Record* and Developing a Rational Response

The purpose of adaptive thinking is to promote optimal thinking when you are feeling stressed. The steps that are involved can be achieved using the rest of the worksheet. Throughout the week when you are feeling stressed, sad, or overwhelmed, continue to list your thoughts for each situation. If you are anticipating a stressful situation, or a task that is making you feel overwhelmed, write out your thoughts regarding this situation. If a situation has already passed, and you find that you are thinking about it negatively, list your thoughts for this situation.

The first column is a description of the situation.

The second column is for you to list your thoughts during a stressful, overwhelming, or uncontrollable situation.

The third column is for you to write down what emotions you are having and what your mood is like when thinking these thoughts (e.g., depressed, sad, angry).

The fourth column is for you to see if your thoughts match the list of thinking errors. These may include the following:

- *All-or-Nothing Thinking*
- *Overgeneralizations*
- *Jumping to Conclusions (Fortune Telling/Mind Reading)*
- *Magnification/Minimization*
- *Emotional Reasoning*
- *"Should" Statements*
- *Labeling and Mislabeling*
- *Personalization*
- *Maladaptive Thinking*
- *Overly Optimistic Thinking*

In the last column, try to come up with a rational response to each thought, or to the most important negative thought. The rational response is a statement that you can say to yourself to try to feel better about the situation. Questions to help come up with this rational response can include the following:

- *What is the evidence that this thought is true?*
- *Is there an alternative explanation?*
- *What is the worst thing that can happen?*
- *Has this situation unreasonably grown in importance?*
- *What would a good coach say about this situation?*
- *Have I done what I can do to control it?*
- *If I were to do anything else, would this help or hinder the situation?*
- *Am I worrying excessively about this?*
- *What would a good friend say to me about this situation?*
- *What would I say to a good friend about this situation if he or she were going through it?*
- *Why is this statement a cognitive distortion?*
- *Is it helpful to focus on this thought at this moment?*

Practice

> *Remember, practicing your new skills will make them feel more comfortable and you will begin to notice improvements. First, identify situations you will work on at home using the thought record. Also consider any difficulties you may have completing this assignment and try to minimize the chance that obstacles will emerge.*

- Continue to use the calendar every day to record appointments and put new tasks on the task list every day.
- Use and look at the task list and calendar EVERY DAY!
- Rate each task as an "A," "B," or "C" task.
- Practice doing all of the "A" tasks before the "B" tasks and all of the "B" tasks before the "C" tasks.
- Carry over tasks that are not completed to the next day's task list.
- Practice using Worksheet 1: *Problem Solving: Selection of Action Plan* for at least one item on the task list.
- Practice breaking down one large task from the task list into smaller steps.
- Use the organizational systems developed in this program.
- Use the distractibility delay when working on boring or unattractive tasks.
- Use your skills to reduce distraction in your work environment.
- Start putting important items in specific places.
- Use reminders to check in with yourself to see if you have become distracted when you are trying to focus on completing a task.
- Read the instructions for completing the *5-Column Thought Record*.
- Complete thought records for at least two situations during the week.

CHAPTER 12: Rehearsal and Review of Adaptive Thinking Skills

OVERVIEW

The primary goal of this chapter is for you to continue working on developing your ability to recognize negative and unhelpful thoughts and changing to more adaptive ways of thinking about situations. You will also begin the process of planning for your use of skills in the future, after you have completed this workbook.

GOALS

- To continue to monitor your progress with the Symptom Checklist
- To review homework from previous modules
- To review use of thought records to develop more adaptive thoughts
- To identify exercises for home practice

Review of Symptom Checklist

As you have been doing each week, complete the ASRS Symptom Checklist at the start of your therapy session, and share this information with your therapist.

Score: _____   Date: _____

Review of Medication Adherence

As you have been doing each week, record your prescribed dosage of medication and indicate the number of doses you missed. List triggers for missed doses.

Prescribed doses per week: _____

Doses missed this week: _____

Triggers for missed doses:

_____

_____

Review of Previous Chapters

Each week you should review your progress implementing skills from each of the previous chapters. It is important to acknowledge the successes you have achieved and try to resolve any difficulties.

Here are the tools for organization and planning:

- Use of calendar for managing appointments: Discuss any problems you are having with using your calendar system.
- Use of task list system: Review any difficulties you are having with using your task list on a daily basis.
- Use of the "A," "B," and "C" priority ratings: Discuss any trouble you are having with prioritizing tasks.
- Use of problem solving (selecting an action plan) and breaking down large tasks into small steps: Consider your use of these strategies and practice one or both skills using examples from your current task list.

Here are the tools for reducing distractibility:

- Use of the strategy of breaking tasks down into manageable chunks: Discuss with your therapist any problems you are having with breaking down tasks.
- Use of the distractibility delay: Review any difficulties you are having with the distractibility delay technique.

- Removing distractions from environment
- Identifying specific places for important items and making sure that the items always get put away in these places
- Use of reminders, "Am I doing what I am supposed to be doing?"

Here are the strategies for developing adaptive thinking:

- Use of thought records to identify and label automatic thoughts
- Use of thought records to identify rational responses

At this point, you may want to discuss any new situations that you are anticipating may require adaptive thinking. Remember to refer to the sections of this workbook on adaptive thinking if you find you are getting stuck. Adaptive thinking is a tool that you can easily use on your own. Initially, it is helpful to write out the five columns and walk yourself through the thought record, but ultimately this process will take place in your mind. With practice, you will learn to spot unhelpful automatic thoughts as they emerge, and you will be able to come up with a rational response to help you feel better about the situation. When necessary, you can always write out the thought record, either on paper (see the *5-Column Thought Record* in the Appendix) or electronically, and review the materials in this workbook.

We suggest using this session to review an additional situation and complete a thought record in full for it.

Planning for Future Parts of Treatment

Congratulations! You have now completed the core elements of cognitive-behavioral treatment for ADHD. Review the "problem list" you completed at the beginning of your treatment to determine whether to do the optional chapter on procrastination or whether to do more review work on chapters you have already completed.

We include one optional chapter on procrastination. The skills you have already learned can be specifically applied to the area of procrastination. It is up to you to figure out if you feel you need the extra work or if it makes more sense to review material already covered in this workbook so far.

Potential Pitfalls

You have done a lot of work to get to this point! You may feel like you want to take a break, or that you have done enough and will no longer have any difficulties related to ADHD. The most important message to remember is that you need to continue to PRACTICE, PRACTICE, PRACTICE! This will ensure that your newly learned skills become permanent. Your effort will continue to pay off.

Practice

- Congratulate yourself for completing the core treatment elements!
- Continue practicing the skills you have learned in previous sections.
- Continue to use your cognitive techniques for situations involving stress.
- Remember to consider any anticipated problems completing the homework.

Additional Skills

MODULE 4

CHAPTER 13: Application of Skills to Procrastination (optional)

OVERVIEW

This session will be helpful if you have been having significant difficulties with procrastination. For adults with ADHD, procrastination can be a result of what we call *cognitive avoidance*—the deliberate postponing of tasks because you can focus more easily when you are closer to the deadline. Procrastinating may also result from perfectionism (thinking the product needs to be perfect, which is not a realistic goal).

The chapter on procrastination consists of a single session because it uses several of the skills you have already learned in previous chapters, including cognitive restructuring of thoughts like, "This paper needs to be perfect or I can't turn it in," breaking down tasks into manageable steps, and learning to set realistic goals for completing individual steps rather than the entire task.

Learning skills for managing procrastination will enable you to do the following:

- Understand the attractive aspects of procrastination
- Anticipate the negative consequences of procrastination
- Use techniques for solving problems related to procrastination
- Use adaptive thinking skills for managing procrastination

GOALS

- To continue to monitor your progress
- To review home practice of previously learned skills
- To learn about the attractiveness and the negative consequences of procrastination
- To use a *Pros and Cons of Procrastination* worksheet to help you decide whether to procrastinate or not
- To adapt problem-solving skills to the issue of procrastination
- To use adaptive thinking for managing procrastination
- To identify areas for home practice

Review of Symptom Checklist

As you have been doing each week, complete the ASRS Symptom Checklist at the start of your therapy session, and share this information with your therapist.

Score: _____   Date: _____

Review of Medication Adherence

As you have been doing each week, record your prescribed dosage of medication and indicate the number of doses you missed. List triggers for missed doses.

Prescribed doses per week: _____

Doses missed this week: _____

Triggers for missed doses:

_____

_____

Review of Previous Chapters

Each week you should review your progress implementing skills from each of the previous chapters. It is important to acknowledge the successes you have achieved and try to resolve any difficulties.

Here are the tools for organization and planning:

- Use of calendar for managing appointments: Discuss any problems you are having with using your calendar system.
- Use of task list system: Review any difficulties you are having with using your task list on a daily basis.
- Use of the "A," "B," and "C" priority ratings: Discuss any trouble you are having with prioritizing tasks.
- Use of problem solving (selecting an action plan) and breaking down large tasks into small steps: Consider your use of these strategies and practice one or both skills using examples from your current task list.

Here are the tools for reducing distractibility:

- Use of the strategy of breaking tasks down into manageable chunks: Discuss with your therapist any problems you are having with breaking down tasks.
- Use of the distractibility delay: Review any difficulties you are having with the distractibility delay technique.
- Removing distractions from environment
- Identifying specific places for important items and making sure that the items always get put away in these places
- Use of reminders, "Am I doing what I am supposed to be doing?"

Here are the strategies for developing adaptive thinking:

- Use of thought records to identify and label automatic thoughts
- Use of thought records to identify rational responses

Introduction to Procrastination

Many individuals with ADHD have struggled with procrastination for quite some time. In this chapter you will review your history with procrastination and try to identify the areas in which it has been most problematic for you. In addition, you will learn to think about the reasons behind your procrastination. Once you discover the reasons, you will be able to use more effective problem-solving strategies that will decrease the interference of procrastination.

The Attractiveness of Procrastination

While procrastination can cause anxiety and anguish, there are also reasons why it *seems* desirable or easier to postpone tasks. Some reasons include these:

- Perfectionism/fear of negative evaluation for a less-than-perfect product
- The idea that it is difficult to get started unless the time pressure is there
- The issue seems overwhelming.
- You have difficulty finding a starting point.
- The tasks requiring sustained effort are not attractive.
- You want to wait for a period when you have enough time (this usually never comes).

Do any of these reasons sound familiar to you? Think about the reasons that seem to underlie procrastination for you. Are there any other reasons that are not listed above?

The Consequences of Procrastination

As discussed above, procrastination can appear to be a good option if it helps you avoid a negative feeling or if you *think* that the time/environment must be just right before you can begin a task. Unfortunately, these potential benefits are often outweighed by far more negative consequences, including the following:

- It is stressful waiting until the last minute to complete a task.
- The task, which is unattractive in the first place, is even worse when it is all-encompassing. (Waiting until the last minute means that you will have to sacrifice other activities near the deadline.)
- There may be times when you miss the deadline and there is a penalty (e.g., lower grade on a paper, boss becomes angry at work).
- You feel worse about yourself later.
- The final product is not as good as it could have been.
- Ignoring the problem usually makes it worse and even harder to solve later.

Do you recognize any of these consequences? Have you experienced them? Think about how procrastination has had negative consequences for you. There may be other negative outcomes that are not listed above but have been significant for you.

Skill: Evaluating the Pros and Cons of Procrastination

Sometimes it can be useful to evaluate the pros and cons of an action before making a decision. In this way, deciding to procrastinate on a task can be seen as a decision that you might be making. Accordingly, you can use a "decisional balance" worksheet to help make a decision about what to do.

Remember that sometimes the short-term pros and cons differ from the long-term ones, so be sure to evaluate both.

Worksheet 8: *Pros and Cons of Procrastination* (in the Appendix) will assist you in objectively rating the pros and cons of procrastination. Think about a situation where you might be tempted to procrastinate. Then fill in the boxes on the worksheet, first writing out the short-term pros and cons, and then writing out the long-term pros and cons. Often, when individuals look at this completed worksheet, they observe that, in the short term, the pros may outweigh the cons, but in the long term, there are more cons.

Unfortunately, it is sometimes difficult to remember the pros and cons in the moment when you are facing an overwhelming task. Taking a time out and reviewing the pros and the cons can be useful at these times.

Skill: Adapting Problem Solving to the Issue of Procrastination

In Chapter 6 of this workbook you also learned to use skills for problem solving. When a task feels overwhelming, or you are uncertain about where to begin, you are more likely to procrastinate. Breaking the task down into manageable steps will help avoid this. Remember that each step should feel completely "do-able." If it doesn't, break the step down further. Alternatively, rather than attempting to work on the whole problem, you may want to target only one or two smaller goals.

Another trap that individuals can fall into is setting unreasonable goals. Recall that each step should be realistic. The skills you learned for managing distractibility will also be useful here. If you know that you are generally able to work on unpleasant tasks for 15 minutes, then you should try to break down each step into goals that can be completed in this timeframe.

Refer back to Worksheet 1: *Problem Solving: Selection of Action Plan* in Chapter 6.

Skill: Using Adaptive Thinking to Help with Procrastination

As you have learned, your thoughts can play a powerful role in how you feel about a situation, and they can influence your actions in a situation. Negative and/or unhelpful automatic thoughts can also greatly contribute to procrastination. Using thought records will help you create balanced, helpful thoughts that will decrease procrastination.

Remember, there are five steps to completing the thought record. You can do this on the form provided (Fig. 13.1) or electronically:

1. List the situation contributing to procrastination.
2. List your automatic thoughts regarding the task or goal.

Time and Situation	Automatic Thoughts	Mood and Intensity	Thinking Error	Rational Response

Figure 13.1

Thought record

3. Identify your feelings connected to the thoughts.
4. Refer to the list of thinking errors to evaluate your thoughts.
5. Formulate rational responses to these thoughts.

As you know, practicing new skills is essential for ultimately being able to use them easily in a given situation. Use these steps:

- Think about a specific task or issue about which you have been procrastinating.
- Specifically use each of the above skills for this task or issue.
- Use the problem-solving strategy to help break the task into manageable steps.
- Write down the steps on your task list.
- Next, list the automatic thoughts you are having about getting started.
- Finally, identify the appropriate thinking errors and try to come up with helpful, rational responses.

Potential Pitfalls

Although you may have struggled with procrastination for many years, it is important to remember that you can use the strategies you have already learned to decrease the interference of procrastination. Even if you are unsure about whether these strategies will help, do an experiment! For one month, commit to using these skills each day, and see how well you do. Chances are, you are going to see the results quickly, and it will then be easier to practice your newly learned techniques.

Practice

- Plan a reasonable goal or two to initiate from the list of steps that you have outlined on your task list.
- Determine a way that you can reward yourself upon completion of the goals.
- Review your use of skills from the previous sections of treatment. Be sure to note any questions or difficulties you may be having.

CHAPTER 14 Handling Slips

Thinking About the End of Treatment

Congratulations! You are now at the end of over a dozen chapters' worth of information and skills designed to help you treat the distress and impairment of your ADHD. However . . .

> **The completion of this workbook and the end of your sessions with your therapist do not equal the end of your program of treatment.**

The strategies and skills that you learned as part of this program now need to be practiced regularly so that they become more automatic. In other words, the end of regular sessions of treatment signifies the starting point of your own program of treatment, where you work to lock in and extend the skills and strategies that you have learned. If you make practice of these skills part of your daily or weekly schedule, you will help ensure that you continue to maintain or extend the benefits you have achieved.

To begin your transition to this next phase of treatment—where you take over the role as the therapist directing your own treatment—it is important for you to recognize the nature of the benefits you have achieved.

Review of Symptom Checklist

As you have been doing each week, complete the ASRS Symptom Checklist at the start of your therapy session, and share this information with your therapist.

Chapter	Score
3	
4	
5	
6	
7	
8	
9	
10	
11	
12	
13	
14	
Other	

Figure 14.1

Symptom scores

Score: _____ Date: _____

Review the symptom scores that you wrote in at the beginning of each chapter with your therapist. You may want to re-copy the scores in Figure 14.1 so that you can see when and where during the course of treatment you made particular gains. Remember, the benefits from any particular treatment strategy may not appear until it has been practiced for several weeks.

Examining What Was Valuable for You

Also, consider what strategies might have been the most useful for you during the program. Worksheet 9: *Treatment Strategies and Usefulness* (in the Appendix) summarizes many of the strategies you have tried.

Rate the usefulness of each strategy to you (0 = didn't help at all to 100 = was extremely important for me). Also, take some time to think about why each strategy worked or didn't work. This will help you identify which strategies might be most helpful for you to practice over the next month.

Maintaining Your Gains

Successful treatment does not mean that you will not have future difficulties with symptoms. For most conditions, symptoms can wax and wane over time.

> **The key to maintaining treatment gains over the long run is to be ready for periods of increased difficulties.**

These periods are not signs that the treatment failed you. Instead, they are signals that you need to apply the skills that you learned in treatment. To help you refresh your skills, study the troubleshooting difficulties chart (Table 14.1). The purpose of the chart is to remind you of the importance of practicing skills, and to help you think through which strategies might be important for you to continue practicing.

The first step in being prepared for this upcoming review is to schedule it. If you followed aspects of this program, you now know exactly where your core calendar is—it is in the location that you identified (and if it isn't there, this might be a first reminder to work harder to always return your important tools to your selected spot). Schedule a review session with yourself one month from the current date. Use Worksheet 10: *One-Month Review* (in the Appendix) for this self-review.

Troubleshooting Your Difficulties

It may also be helpful to match some of the symptoms you may be experiencing with some of the specific strategies used in treatment. Examine the chart in Table 14.1, and see if it helps you identify some of the strategies that may be helpful to practice.

Table 14.1 Troubleshooting Difficulties Chart

Symptoms	Skills to Consider
Failing to give adequate attention to details/making careless mistakes in work or other activities	Recheck your attention span and your ability to break activities into units where you can sustain attention. Use your cues (alarm) to remind you of core responsibilities at hand.
Difficulty sustaining attention in tasks	Check your management of your space. Are your environments too distracting?
Difficulty organizing tasks in terms of importance	Use your prioritization system. Use your triage and organizational systems.
Procrastination	Use problem solving and adaptive thinking. Break down large tasks into smaller steps.
Losing things necessary for tasks or activities	Use a single work area. Use your triage and organizational systems. Work with another person to reduce clutter.
Easily distracted by things going on in the environment	Manage your environment, and use your distractibility delay.
Forgetful in daily activities	Use your alarm system and your task list along with your calendar.

Finally, you may want to use Worksheet 1: *Problem Solving: Selection of Action Plan* in Chapter 6 to more carefully consider any difficulties with symptoms you are currently having. And if these strategies do not help, consider getting additional input from family or friends, or schedule a booster session with your therapist.

We wish you the best in continuing to use these skills!

Appendix

Forms and Worksheets

Accessing Treatments *ThatWork* Forms and Worksheets Online

All forms and worksheets from books in the TTW series are made available digitally shortly following print publication. You may download, print, save, and digitally complete them as PDFs. To access the forms and worksheets, please visit http://www.oup.com/us/ttw.

Worksheet 1: Problem-Solving: Selection of Action Plan

Worksheet 2: Steps for Sorting Mail

Worksheet 3: Developing an Organizational System

Worksheet 4: Strategies for Reducing Distractions

Worksheet 5: 3-Column Thought Record

Handout A: Preliminary Instructions for Adaptive Thinking

Worksheet 6: 4-Column Thought Record

Handout B: Instructions for Completing a 5-Column Thought Record and Developing a Rational Response

Worksheet 7: 5-Column Thought Record

Worksheet 8: Pros and Cons of Procrastination

Worksheet 9: Treatment Strategies and Usefulness

Worksheet 10: One-Month Review

Worksheet 1 Problem-Solving: Selection of Action Plan

Statement of the Problem: _____

_____

_____

Instructions for completing this chart:

1) List all of the possible solutions that you can think of for resolving the problem listed above. List solutions even if you think they don't make sense, or you don't think you would do them. The point is to come up with AS MANY solutions AS POSSIBLE.
2) Make sure that continuing what you are doing now (e.g., avoiding, or doing nothing, if that is the case) is one of the possible solutions.
3) List the pros and cons of each solution.
4) After listing the pros and cons of each, give a rating to each solution on a 1–10 scale, with 1 being the worst and 10 being the best, based on your assessment of the pros and cons of each solution.
5) Use additional copies of this sheet as needed (even if it's for the same problem).

Possible Solution	Pros of Solution	Cons of Solution	Overall Rating of Solution (1–10)

Worksheet 2   Steps for Sorting Mail

1. Identify a central location for your triage center: This is where you will open and sort all incoming mail, bills, and paperwork. You can use a wicker basket, file tray, drawer, bowl, or box for this purpose. The location should be close to your recycling bin and your shredder so that you can recycle junk mail immediately and shred items, such as credit card offers, that have personal information but do not need to be retained. Your goal is to keep only the minimum amount of paper needed. It can be helpful to "unsubscribe" to email lists or opt out of mailing lists to reduce the amount of electronic and paper mail that is coming in.

    Receptacle you will use for your triage center _____

    Central location for your triage center _____

2. Figure out "rules" regarding keeping mail, bills, and paperwork (e.g., I will save copies of all bills for six months after they have been paid; I will pay bills right away). If you have a scanner, you may want to scan items and discard the originals to reduce clutter. One item on your task list may be to purchase or set up a scanner and test out the process. Alternatively, you may take a picture with your phone and transfer the photo to a folder on your computer for important documents. Write in your rules below:

    _____

    _____

    _____

    _____

3. Gather all necessary items to keep with triage center: Most tasks can be completed on the computer, so you should have your computer or tablet nearby when you are triaging. If you cannot pay a bill or otherwise respond to an item online, you should keep your checkbook, stamps, pens, calculator, address book, and so on nearby so that you don't need to go searching for these items when you need to pay a bill or respond to a letter.

4. Identify two or three times per week when you will go through the items in the triage center and take any action that is required (pay bill, make phone call, respond to letter, and so on). Use your calendar and task list to help with planning (e.g., put the task of going through mail on your task list).

5. Write your "triage times" in your calendar. Choose times when you will have enough time to deal with all of the items; avoid times when you will be too tired or stressed to be effective at this task.

6. If you experience negative thoughts and you want to give up, try not to give in to this impulse. You will learn how to cope with negative thoughts in the upcoming module on adaptive thinking.

Worksheet 3 Developing an Organizational System

Organizational System for: _____

1. Decide where you will keep your system. (Don't spend too much time making this decision.) If the system is for paper or objects, this can be an actual location. If it is for computerized files, it can be a folder or drive on your computer.

2. Decide on categories. For example, if you are organizing tax information on your computer, you may want to set up a folder for each year and then make sub-folders for various deductions. If you are organizing your clothes in your closet, you may decide to put all of your shirts together, your pants together, and so on.

3. Buy any materials that you need for your system (file folders for a physical filing system, hangers for your closet, baskets or bins if you are organizing smaller items, etc.).

4. Set up your main categories. You can always break down the categories further as you go along if needed. Try to keep the system as simple as possible. As the system becomes more complicated, the likelihood that you will use it becomes lower.

5. Start sorting your items into categories. It is important to use the OHIO (Only Handle It Once) method. This means that when you pick up an item, you decide what to do with it immediately (put it away in final destination—file, closet, or wherever, donate it, shred it, recycle it, throw it away, or delete it). You should never have a category called "decide what to do with this later."

6. If it is too overwhelming to deal with everything at once, use the strategy of breaking tasks down into smaller chunks described earlier. You can chunk it by setting a time goal (e.g., work on the organizational system for 20 minutes), an item goal (e.g., "I will deal with the first 20 pieces of paper I touch," "I will sort through 50 emails"), or a section goal (e.g., "I will sort all of my folded sweaters"). Once you complete this "chunk," you may feel a sense of accomplishment and/or you may realize that it is not going to be as time-consuming as you imagined to set up your organizational system.

7. Plan specific times each week that you will use the system. Make sure you are not choosing unrealistic times.

8. Remember that it is important to practice these skills for long enough that they become a habit. Don't give up too soon! It may have taken a long time for the current disorganized state to come into being, so don't expect yourself to become perfectly organized overnight.

9. Reward yourself for using the system!

Worksheet 4

Strategies for Reducing Distractions

Distraction	Environmental Reduction Strategy

Worksheet 5

3-Column Thought Record

Time and Situation	Automatic Thoughts	Mood and Intensity

Handout A

Preliminary Instructions for Adaptive Thinking

The purpose of using thought records is to identify and modify negative, automatic thoughts in situations that lead to feeling overwhelmed.

The first step in learning to think in more useful ways is to become more aware of these thoughts and their relationship to your feelings. If you are anticipating a stressful situation, or a task that is making you feel overwhelmed, write out your thoughts regarding this situation.

If a situation has already passed and you find that you are thinking about it negatively or if, in retrospect, you realize that you were having unhelpful thoughts, list your thoughts for this situation.

The first column is a description of the situation.

The second column is for you to list your thoughts during a stressful, overwhelming, or uncontrollable situation.

The third column is for you to write down what emotions or feelings you are having when thinking these thoughts (e.g., depressed, sad, angry).

The fourth column is for you to see if your thoughts match the list of "thinking errors." These may include:

- *All-or-Nothing Thinking*
- *Overgeneralizations*
- *Jumping to Conclusions (Fortune Telling/Mind Reading)*
- *Magnification/Minimization*
- *Emotional Reasoning*
- *"Should" Statements*
- *Labeling and Mislabeling*
- *Personalization*
- *Maladaptive Thinking*
- *Overly Optimistic Thinking*

Worksheet 6

4-Column Thought Record

Time and Situation	Automatic Thoughts	Mood and Intensity	Thinking Errors

Handout B

Instructions for Completing the 5-Column thought Record and Developing a Rational Response

The purpose of adaptive thinking is to promote optimal thinking when you are feeling stressed. The steps that are involved can be achieved using the rest of the worksheet. Throughout the week when you are feeling stressed, sad, or overwhelmed, continue to list your thoughts for each situation. If you are anticipating a stressful situation or a task that is making you feel overwhelmed, write out your thoughts regarding this situation. If a situation has already passed and you find that you are thinking about it negatively, list your thoughts for this situation.

The first column is a description of the situation.

The second column is for you to list your thoughts during a stressful, overwhelming, or uncontrollable situation.

The third column is for you to write down what emotions you are having and what your mood is like when thinking these thoughts (e.g., depressed, sad, angry).

The fourth column is for you to see if your thoughts match the list of "thinking errors" These may include:

- *All-or-Nothing thinking*
- *Overgeneralizations*
- *Jumping to Conclusions (Fortune Telling/Mind Reading)*
- *Magnification/Minimization*
- *Emotional Reasoning*
- *"Should" Statements*
- *Labeling and Mislabeling*
- *Personalization*
- *Maladaptive Thinking*
- *Overly Optimistic Thinking*

In the last column, try to come up with a rational response to each thought, or to the most important negative thought. The rational response is a statement that you can say to yourself to try to feel better about the situation. Questions to help come up with this rational response can include the following:

- *What is the evidence that this thought is true?*
- *Is there an alternative explanation?*
- *What is the worst thing that can happen?*
- *Has this situation unreasonably grown in importance?*
- *What would a good coach say about this situation?*
- *Have I done what I can do to control it?*
- *If I were to do anything else, would this help or hinder the situation?*
- *Am I worrying excessively about this?*
- *What would a good friend say to me about this situation?*
- *What would I say to a good friend about this situation if he or she were going through it?*
- *Why is this statement a cognitive distortion?*
- *Is it helpful to focus on this thought at this moment?*

Worksheet 7 5-Column Thought Record

Time and Situation	Automatic Thoughts	Mood and Intensity	Thinking Errors	Rational Response
What is the evidence for the thought? Against the thought? Why is it the particular cognitive distortion? Is there an alternate explanation? What is the worst thing that could happen? What would a good friend or good coach say? What would you say to a friend in a similar situation?					

Worksheet 8

Pros and Cons of Procrastination

	Pros	Cons
Short-term		
Long-term		

Worksheet 9   Treatment Strategies and Usefulness

Please rate the usefulness of each strategy to you ("0" = Didn't help at all to "100" = Was extremely important for me). Also, take some time to provide notes to yourself about why you think each strategy worked or didn't work to help you, and formulate a plan regarding which strategies might be most helpful for you to practice over the next month.

Treatment Strategies	Usefulness Ratings	Notes About Your Application/ Usefulness of the Strategy
Tools for Organization and Planning • Use of calendar for managing appointments • Use of task list • Use of strategy for breaking down tasks into subtasks • Use of A-B-C ratings for prioritizing multiple tasks • Use of problem-solving and developing an action plan • Use of triage and organizational systems Strategies for Managing Distractibility • Use of strategy for breaking down tasks into duration of attention span and use of breaks in between tasks • Using distractibility delay • Removing distractions from environment • Identifying specific places for important objects • Use of reminders: alarm, "Am I doing what I am supposed to be doing?" Adaptive Thinking • Use of thought records to identify negative thoughts • Reviewing list of thinking errors • Use of thought records to create balanced, helpful thoughts		

Worksheet 10

One-Month Review

Date of review: _____

1. What skills have you been practicing well?

2. Where do you still have troubles?

3. Can you place the troubles in one of the specific domains used in this treatment?

4. Have you reviewed the chapters most relevant to your difficulties? (Which chapters are these?)

5. Have you reviewed Worksheet 9: *Treatment Strategies and Usefulness*, where you wrote those skills that were most helpful to you in the first phase of this treatment? Do you need to reapply these skills or strategies?

References

American Psychiatric Association. (2013). *Diagnostic and statistical manual of mental disorders* (5th ed.). Washington, DC: American Psychiatric Association.

Barkley, R. A. (1998). *Attention-deficit hyperactivity disorder: A handbook for diagnosis and treatment* (2nd ed.). New York: Guilford Press.

Craske, M. H., & Barlow, D. H. (2006). *Mastery of your anxiety and worry: Client workbook* (2nd ed.). New York: Oxford.

D'Zurilla, T. J. (1986). *Problem-solving therapy: A social competence approach to clinical interventions.* New York: Springer.

Hallowell, E. M. (1995). Psychotherapy of adult attention deficit disorder. In K. G. Nadeau (Ed.), *A comprehensive guide to attention deficit disorder in adults: Research, diagnosis, and treatment* (pp. 146–167). New York: Brunner/Mazel.

Hope, D. A., Heimberg, R. H., Juster, H. R., & Turk, C. L. (2000). *Managing social anxiety: A cognitive behavioral therapy approach.* Boulder, CO: Graywind Publications.

Kelly, K., & Ramundo, P. (1993). *You mean I'm not lazy, stupid, or crazy? A self-help book for adults with attention deficit disorder.* New York: Fireside.

Mayes, V. (1998). *A clinician's handbook for attention-deficit hyperactivity disorder in adults.* Unpublished dissertation, Colorado State University.

McDermott, S. P. (2000). Cognitive therapy of adults with attention-deficit/hyperactivity disorder. In T. Brown (Ed.), *Attention deficit disorders and comorbidity in children, adolescents, and adults.* Washington, DC: American Psychiatric Press.

Nadeau, K. G. (1995). Life management skills for the adult with ADD. In K. G. Nadeau (Ed.), *A comprehensive guide to attention deficit disorder in adults: Research, diagnosis, and treatment* (pp. 191–217). New York: Brunner/Mazel.

Nezu, A. M., Nezu, C. M., Friedman, S. H., Faddis, S., & Houts, P. S. (1998). *Helping cancer patients cope: A problem-solving approach.* Washington, DC: American Psychological Association.

Otto, M. W., Jones, J. C., Craske, M. G., & Barlow, D. H. (1996). *Stopping anxiety medication: Panic control therapy for benzodiazepine discontinuation (therapist guide).* San Antonio, TX: Psychological Corporation.

Safren, S. A., Sprich, S., Chulvick, S., & Otto, M. W. (2004). Psychosocial treatments for adults with ADHD. *Psychiatric Clinics of North America, 27*(2), 349–360.

Safren, S. A., Otto, M. W., Sprich, S. E., Winett, C. L., Wilens, T. E., & Biederman, J. (2005). Cognitive-Behavioral Therapy for ADHD in medication-treated adults with continued symptoms. *Behaviour Research and Therapy, 43*(7), 831–842.

Safren, S. A., Sprich, S., Mimiaga, M. J., Surman, C., Knouse, L., Groves, M., & Otto, M. W. (2010). Cognitive behavioral therapy vs. relaxation with educational support for medication-treated adults with ADHD and persistent symptoms: A randomized controlled trial. *JAMA, 304*(8), 875–880.

About the Authors

Steven A. Safren, PhD, is currently a Professor of Psychology at the University of Miami. His grant-funded work related to ADHD includes being the principal investigator (PI) of a five-year NIMH R01 to study the efficacy of cognitive-behavioral therapy (CBT) for ADHD in adults, and the lead author of the outcome of that trial published in *JAMA—the Journal of the American Medical Association*. He was also the PI of a two-year NIMH R03 that studied the initial efficacy of CBT for ADHD in adults, and multiple PI (with Dr. Sprich) of a three-year R34 to examine the efficacy of this approach with adolescents. Before working at the University of Miami, Dr. Safren was, for 18 years, at the Department of Psychiatry at Massachusetts General Hospital (MGH)/Harvard Medical School, where he was a Professor of Psychology and Director of Behavioral Medicine. There he served in a variety of other roles, such as the Director for the Cognitive Behavioral Therapy and Behavioral Medicine Clinical Psychology Internship tracks, and as the Associate Director of the Cognitive Behavioral Therapy Program. Additionally, he maintained a clinical practice treating clients with CBT at MGH. At the time of writing, Dr. Safren has over 250 publications in the areas of CBT, psychopathology, and their application to a variety of clinical problems in adults. In addition to his focus on adult ADHD, Dr. Safren has a major focus working on the development and testing of interventions related to medical problems such as HIV. This work is also funded by the National Institutes of Health.

Susan E. Sprich, PhD, is the Director of the Cognitive Behavioral Therapy Program at MGH and an Assistant Professor in Psychology at Harvard Medical School. She also serves as the Director of Postgraduate Psychology Education at the Psychiatry Academy at MGH. She was the Project Director of a five-year study of CBT for adult ADHD and the co-PI of a three-year study of CBT for adolescent ADHD, both funded by NIMH. She is also involved in clinical research in the treatment of Obsessive-Compulsive Disorder, Autism Spectrum Disorders, trichotillomania, and other anxiety and mood disorders. She has authored over 20 publications in the areas of ADHD and anxiety disorders in children and adults. Dr. Sprich conducts CBT with clients with mood disorders, anxiety disorders, and ADHD through the Cognitive Behavioral Therapy Program at MGH and in private practice. Dr. Sprich received her doctorate in clinical psychology from the State University of New York at Albany, and did her predoctoral and postdoctoral fellowships in CBT at MGH/Harvard Medical School.

Carol A. Perlman, PhD, is a Cognitive Behavioral Therapist who specializes in the treatment of mood disorders, anxiety disorders, and adult ADHD. Dr. Perlman was formerly a Clinical Assistant in Psychology at MGH, Instructor in Psychology at Harvard Medical School, and Project Director at the Harvard University Department of Psychology. She received her doctorate in clinical psychology from the University of Miami in Coral Gables, Florida, and her postdoctoral training at MGH/Harvard Medical School. She served as a therapist for the initial study of CBT for adult ADHD and a Co-Investigator and therapist for the efficacy study. Dr. Perlman has published over 20 articles in the area of mood disorders, posttraumatic stress disorder, and adult ADHD. She is a national workshop presenter on CBT. Dr. Perlman is the owner of Perlman Psychology Associates, LLC and maintains a private practice in Medway, Massachusetts.

Michael W. Otto, PhD, is Professor of Psychological and Brain Sciences at Boston University. He specializes in CBT of anxiety, mood, and substance use disorders. He has had a major career focus on developing and validating new psychosocial treatments, including treatments for ADHD. His research includes a translational research agenda investigating brain–behavior relationships in therapeutic learning, including the use of novel medications (e.g., D-cycloserine, yohimbine) and novel behavioral strategies to improve therapeutic learning/outcome. His focus on hard-to-treat conditions and principles underlying behavior-change failures led him to an additional focus on health behavior promotion, including investigations of addictive behaviors, medication adherence, sleep, smoking, and exercise. Across these health behaviors, he has been concerned with cognitive, attention, and affective factors that derail adaptive behaviors, and the factors that can rescue these processes. Dr. Otto has over 370 publications spanning his research interests and was identified as a "top producer" in the clinical empirical literature. Dr. Otto is a past President of the Association for Behavioral and Cognitive Therapies, a member of the Scientific Advisory Board for the Anxiety and Depression Association of America, and President Elect of the Society for Clinical Psychology.

Made in United States
Troutdale, OR
06/01/2024

20251313R00071